Published by

MAPQUEST

Copyright © 2005
by MapQuest, Inc.
All rights reserved.

Acknowledgements:
"How to use this Atlas", written by Elspeth Leacock.

Mexico State coat of arms on page 76, © 2005 mexican-flag.com

Photographs on pages 24–25 (Deserts, Nature, China/Tibet, Alaska, Brazil, Arctic), 26–27 (Landscapes, Nature, Australia, China/ Tibet), 59 (rivers), 60–61(nature, Landscapes, Hawaii, Caribbean), 62–63 (Arctic) Copyright © 2005 Corel corp. and their suppliers.

Photographs on pages 26–27 (Vol.16, 44, 74), 60–61 (Vol. 16, 44), 62–63 (Vol. 16, 44) Copyright © 2005 PhotoDisc, Inc.

Photograph on page 42 (Wright brother's flight) Copyright © 2005 NASA

Photographs on pages 58, 62–63 (Southern California) Copyright © 2005 Digital Stock Corp.

Photograph on page 62 (Rockiespring) Copyright © 2005 Freestockphotos.com

Photographs on pages 68–69 (Vol. 194) Copyright © 2005 Corbis Corp.

AN ATLAS is a collection of maps that can be
used to find information about your world. The
very latest data has been collected to make these
maps. Hundreds of satellite images were used to
map the dramatic shrinking of Earth's forests.
The latest census data from each and every country was used to build a picture of Earth's current
population. The most recent scientific research
was used to create thematic maps of continental
drift, the ocean floor, the environment and our
natural resources. Look closely and you will see
that the information for the maps comes from
many different sources such as NASA, the U.S.
Department of the Interior or the World Bank.
You can use these maps to explore your world,
discover connections between places, and see
relationships between places and peoples.

But this atlas is more than just a wealth of
information. It is fun to look at too. You will
find that these maps and photographs can evoke
images of far away places. They invite you to
pause and to dream. With a map you can journey
the world without ever getting wet, cold, tired or
hungry. You can imagine great adventures and
not leave the comfort of your favorite chair!

To get the most out of this atlas you need to
know how to read maps. Just as you learned to
read words like the ones on this page, you can
learn how to read the language of maps. The
map skills you need to know are:
1. locating places
2. measuring distance
3. finding direction
4. reading map symbols

Locating Places
To find places in this atlas, you can begin with
the index. To find Dallas follow these steps.

1. Look up Dallas in the index at the
   end of this book.
2. The index tells you that Dallas is a
   city in Texas and that it can be
   found on page 50. You will also
   learn that Dallas is located at
   32°47'N (32 degrees 47 minutes
   north) and 96°48'W (96 degrees 48
   minutes west.)
3. Go to page 50 and find the line of
   latitude nearest to the number
   32°N and the line of longitude
nearest to the number 96°W. You will find
Dallas close to where those two lines meet. You
can learn more about latitude and longitude on
pages 8–9.

Measuring Distance
To measure distance most maps have a distance
scale. You can learn more about measuring distance on page 7.

Finding Direction

To find directions use the map's compass rose.
You can also use lines of latitude and longitude
to find direction. Every line of longitude points
north and south. Every line of latitude points
east and west. You can learn more about latitude
and longitude on pages 8–9.

Reading Map Symbols

Every map symbol shows the location of something. It could be something as large as a continent or as small as a bird-house. A dot
shows the location of a city. A blue line
shows the course of a river. But map
symbols are not the same on all maps.
One map might show a city with a
square. Map legends or keys help
explain the symbols used on a map.
You can find out more about legends
and the map symbols used in this atlas
on page 6.

Special Features of this Atlas

This atlas has been designed and organized to be
easy for you to use. Here is a "road map" to your
atlas.

The Blue Tab Bar
Somewhere along the top blue tab bar of each
spread you will see a darker blue tab. It tells you

| Geographic Features | **Climate** | Land Cover |

the subject of the map or maps you are looking
at. The light blue tabs tell you the subjects of the
surrounding map spreads. If, for example, you
are looking at the World Climate map and would
like to compare it to the World Vegetation map,
you can use the tabs to find that map quickly
and easily.

Map Skills
Look at the blue tab bar above and you will see
that you are in the map skills section. This section should be called "Read Me First" because it
is here that you will find all sorts of helpful
information about maps and how to read them.
Even if you are a practiced map reader, read this
section!

The World
In this section you will find a world political
map, a world physical map, and 35 world thematic maps. The world political map shows the
most up to date national boundaries. On the
world physical map you can see huge deserts,

great mountain ranges, and even the sea ice that covers much of the Arctic. The thematic maps include the most up to date information on everything from the world distribution of computers and televisions to life expectancy, religion and literacy. If you want to see the ocean floor, or to find where in the world volcanoes form, this is the section to look in.

Continents

The continent units are designed to all have the same kinds of maps. This will enable you to compare and contrast one continent with another with ease and accuracy. There is a political map, a physical map, and a total of seven thematic maps per continent.

Used individually each map can provide answers to many questions. But all together, each set of maps can be used to tell a story.

Imagine a journey crossing a continent. You can see the regions visited, the mountains climbed, or the deserts crossed. You can tell if many people are passed along the way or few. You can describe the activities of the people. Will you see miners or ranchers or farmers? And you can tell about the different climates experienced along the way. All of this information and more is on the maps for every continent but Antarctica.

Environmental Issues

There is a special "Environmental Issues" feature for each continent and one for the world. To create these features the latest scientific information was gathered and organized for you. The topics cover the three major environmental issues faced by citizens today, desertification, deforestation, and acid rain.

The United States

In the section on the United States you will find a political map with two pages of political facts, a physical map with two pages of physical facts, and seven thematic map spreads.

Canada and Mexico

Canada and Mexico both have their own spreads that include a political and physical map.

Geographic Features

There are two special "Geographic Features" included in this atlas. To find out how the continents, Earth's greatest land features, have been drifting around the globe, turn to pages 22–23. To take an in depth look at fall lines, divides, and faults turn to the United States Geographic Features spread on pages 58–59.

Charts and Graphs

This atlas is filled with charts, graphs and diagrams. They are used to give more information about subjects shown on the maps. To make these charts and graphs, long lists of the most up to date data was gathered. Then all those numbers were organized into graphic displays that can be read simply and accurately.

Line graphs are used to show change in amounts over time.

Bar graphs are used to compare amounts.

Pie charts show percentages of a total.

Glossary

There are many geographic terms found on maps such as *fjord, isthmus,* or *plateau.* You can find the meaning of these and other terms in the geographic glossary located on the inside back cover.

The staff at Mapquest worked hard to make this atlas a reference book that is both full of information and fun and easy to use. We hope that you enjoy your copy.

Legend

The following symbols are used here for general reference maps. Maps with special subjects (thematic maps) have their own unique legends.

General Reference Maps

- ⊛ National capital
- ★ Other capital
- • Other city
- International boundary (political map)
- International boundary in dispute/undefined (political map)
- State or provincial boundary
- International boundary (physical map)
- International boundary in dispute (physical map)

- Nonsubject area
- ▲ Mountain peak
- ▽ Lowest point
- Perennial lake
- Intermittent lake
- Perennial river
- ≈ Falls

Physical Maps Legend

Pack ice — Ice caps
Mountains — Tundra
Oceans and seas — Forests
Arid lands — Grasslands

Projections

A globe is the most accurate picture of the Earth. Only a globe can show distance, direction, and the true shape and area of land and sea. Mapmakers struggle with how to show the round world on a flat map.

Imagine the Earth as a large balloon.

Cut it apart, and flatten it to make a map.

To show the round Earth on flat paper, mapmakers used different **projections**, or ways of showing a round shape on a flat surface.

With every projection the shapes of places are changed somewhat. This is called distortion. To find distortion, you can compare the latitude and longitude lines of a map to those same lines on a globe.

Mercator Projection

Gerardus Mercator, a Dutch mapmaker, wanted a map projection that showed direction and shape accurately. The problems with distortions are more obvious on this projection. You can see that the land areas are very distorted the closer to the poles that you get. So, this projection ended up greatly distorting distance and size.

This diagram shows how a Mercator projection distorts the sizes of places. Compare Greenland on the map and the globe.

Projections – Making the Round World Flat

Robinson Projection

Arthur Robinson, an American mapmaker, wanted to develop a map projection that "looked" right. This projection uses many distortions but none are significant. You can see this by comparing one of the large scale World maps in this atlas to a globe.

Azimuthal Projection

This is a projection used to show Antarctica and the Arctic. Azimuthal maps show direction and distance accurately, if measured from the center of the map. But, other distances, shape and size are distorted.

Map Scale

Changing Scale

The **large scale map** of New York's lower Manhattan (top) shows a small area with a large amount of detail. The **small scale map** of New York State (bottom) is a large area with a small amount of detail.

0   1   2 miles

0   1   2
inches

One inch represents 1 mile

0   10   20   30   40   50 kilometers

0   1   2   3   4   5
centimeters

One centimeter represents 10 kilometers

The map of metropolitan New York (left) covers an area nearly 50 times larger than the map of lower Manhattan, above.

ATLANTIC OCEAN

The map of New York State (left) covers an area over 112 times larger than the metro New York map above, and 5,243 times the area of the lower Manhattan map.

Latitude and Longitude

Since ancient times, mapmakers, geographers, and navigators have worked to develop a system for accurately locating places on the Earth. On a sphere, such as the Earth, there are no corners or sides, no beginning or end. But since the Earth rotates on an axis, there are two fixed points: the North Pole and the South Pole. These points make a good starting place for a system of imaginary lines.

These imaginary lines form a grid over the Earth, allowing us to pinpoint the exact location of any spot on the Earth. This spherical grid is called the **graticule**. It is formed by lines called **latitude** and **longitude**.

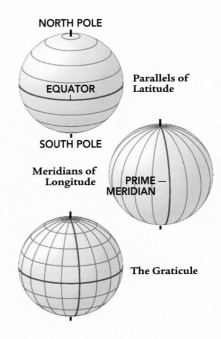

NORTH POLE

EQUATOR

SOUTH POLE

Parallels of Latitude

Meridians of Longitude

PRIME MERIDIAN

The Graticule

Latitude

NORTH POLE
90°N
60°N   60°N
30°N   30°N
90°   30°
EQUATOR 0°   0°
90°
30°S   30°S
60°S   60°S
90°S
SOUTH POLE

Halfway between the poles the equator circles the globe in an east-west direction. Latitude is measured in degrees north or south of the equator, which is 0 degrees (°). Lines of latitude are called **parallels** because they circle the globe parallel to the equator. Parallels are numbered from 0° at the Equator to 90°N at the North Pole and 90°S at the South Pole.

Longitude

Running from pole to pole, lines of longitude—called **meridians**—circle the globe in a north-south direction. As in any circle or sphere, there are 360 degrees (°) of longitude. The meridians are numbered from the Prime Meridian which is labeled 0°. Meridians east or west of the Prime Meridian are labeled E or W up to 180°. The International Date Line generally follows the 180° meridian, making a few jogs to avoid cutting through land areas.

180°
150°W   150°E
120°W   120°E
180°
90°W   90°E
90°
Prime Meridian
60°W   60°E
30°W   30°E
0°

0°
Prime Meridian

180°
International Date Line

Parallels and Meridians—The Facts

Parallels
- are lines of latitude used to measure location north or south of the Equator
- are always the same distance apart (about 70 miles)
- differ in length
- The Equator, the longest parallel, is almost 25,000 miles long

Meridians
- are lines of longitude used to measure location east or west of the Prime Meridian
- meet at the poles
- are all the same length

Which way north...

The geographic North and South Poles are fixed points located at each end of the Earth's axis. The Earth's magnetic fields cause the needle of a compass to point toward magnetic north, not geographic north. The north magnetic pole is located in the northern territories of Canada. The south magnetic pole is located near the coast of Antarctica. The magnetic poles are constantly moving.

Degrees, Minutes, Seconds

A degree (°) of latitude or longitude can be divided into 60 parts called minutes ('). Each minute can be divided into 60 seconds ("). The diagram at right is an example of a place located to the nearest second.

It is written as:
42° 21' 30" N   71° 03' 37" W

- This place is city center, Boston, Massachusetts.

The index at the back of this Atlas uses degrees and minutes of latitude and longitude to help you find places.

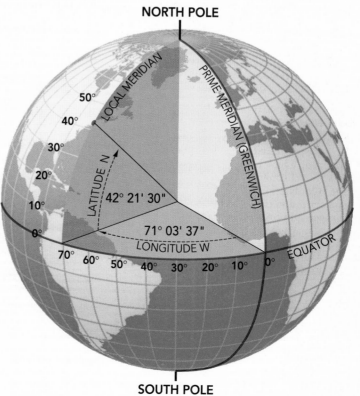

Different Kinds of Maps

Maps are special pictures of places on Earth.

All maps are alike in these important ways:
- All maps are a view from above
- All maps show selected information using symbols
- All maps are smaller than the real place on Earth that they show.

Because people want to show many different things on Earth, they create many different kinds of maps.

Physical Maps

The purpose of a physical map is to show the physical or natural World. Physical maps show landforms and bodies of water. We use physical maps to locate rivers and mountains, ocean currents and wind patterns.

Political Maps

The purpose of a political map is to show the political divisions that people have made on the Earth. Political maps show the boundaries of nations and states and the location of towns and cities. We use political maps to locate places where people live and to understand how human beings have divided up the Earth.

hematic, or Special Purpose Maps

These maps show a specific subject (theme) or very limited number of subjects (such as population density, climate or historical topics). They can be used to show distributions and relationships among map features. This page contains examples of the many types of maps to be found throughout the *Student Atlas of the World.*

Locator

Robinson Projection

NORTH AMERICA · EUROPE · ASIA · ATLANTIC OCEAN · AFRICA · PACIFIC OCEAN · Equator · SOUTH AMERICA · INDIAN OCEAN · AUSTRALIA · PACIFIC OCEAN · ANTARCTICA

Population Density Map

Climate Map

Historic Route Map

Gross Domestic Product (GDP) Map

Land Use Map

Vegetation Map

Continental Drift Map

ICELAND · NORWAY · SWEDEN · FINLAND · ESTONIA · LATVIA · LITHUANIA · DENMARK · IRELAND · UNITED KINGDOM · NETHERLANDS · BELGIUM · GERMANY · POLAND · BELARUS · LUXEMBOURG · UKRAINE · LIECHT. · CZECH REP. · SLOVAKIA · MOLDOVA · FRANCE · SWITZ. · AUSTRIA · HUNGARY · SLOVENIA · ROMANIA · PORTUGAL · ANDORRA · ITALY · CROATIA · BOS. & HER. · SERB. & MONT. · GEORGIA · ARMENIA · AZERBAIJAN · SPAIN · F.Y.R. MACEDONIA · ALBANIA · TURKEY · GIBRALTAR (U.K.) · GREECE · MALTA

AUSTRALIA · Brisbane · Southport · Gold Coast · Newcastle · Sydney · Adelaide · Canberra · Melbourne · Tasmania · Hobart · Greenland (Kalaallit Nunaat) (Den.) · Nuuk · CANADA · St. John's · Minneapolis · New York · th Valley · est recorded perature: 134°F (57°C), 1913 · UNITED STATES · Phoenix · Atlanta · MEXICO · Mexico City · THE BAHAMAS · CUBA · HAITI · JAMAICA · ST. KITTS & NEVIS · Puerto Rico (U.S.) · San Juan · DOMINICAN REPUBLIC · ST. LUCIA · DOMINICA · BARBADOS · ST. VINCENT & THE GRENADINES · ANTIGUA & BARBUDA · GRENADA · TRINIDAD & TOBAGO · BELIZE · HONDURAS · GUATEMALA · NICARAGUA · San José · EL SALVADOR · COSTA RICA · PANAMA

Tangier · Rabat · Algiers · Constantine · Tunis · TUNISIA · Casablanca · Oran · Tripoli · Benghazi · MOROCCO · Alexandria · Western Sahara (Morocco) · ALGERIA · LIBYA · Cairo · EGYPT · CAPE VERDE · MAURITANIA · MALI · NIGER · CHAD · Khartoum · ERITREA · Massawa · Dakar · SENEGAL · BURKINA FASO · SUDAN · Addis Ababa · DJIBOUTI · GAMBIA · GUINEA-BISSAU · GUINEA · BENIN · NIGERIA · Conakry · GHANA · TOGO · Lagos · ETHIOPIA · SIERRA LEONE · Abidjan · CENTRAL AFRICAN REPUBLIC · SOMALIA · LIBERIA · CÔTE D'IVOIRE · EQUATORIAL GUINEA · CAMEROON · Kisangani · UGANDA · KENYA · SAO TOME AND PRINCIPE · GABON · REP. OF THE CONGO · Kampala · Kisumu · Nairobi · Pointe-Noire · DEM. REP. OF THE CONGO · RWANDA · BURUNDI · Mombasa · Cabinda (Angola) · Kinshasa · TANZANIA · Dar-es-Salaam · SEYCHELLES · ANGOLA · Likasi · COMOROS · Lubumbashi · MALAWI · Mayotte (France) · ZAMBIA · MOZAMBIQUE · MADAGASCAR · MAURITIUS · NAMIBIA · Harare · ZIMBABWE · Pretoria · SWAZILAND · BOTSWANA · Johannesburg · Durban · SOUTH AFRICA · LESOTHO · Cape Town · Port Elizabeth

VENEZUELA · SURINAME · FRENCH GUIANA (Fr.) · COLOMBIA · GUYANA · ECUADOR · BRAZIL · PERU · BOLIVIA · CHILE · PARAGUAY · URUGUAY · ARGENTINA

ARCTIC OCEAN · Greenland · NORTH AMERICA · EUROPE · ASIA · PACIFIC OCEAN · TURKEY · ARABIA · PHILIPPINES · SOUTH AMERICA · AFRICA · INDIA · NEW GUINEA · MADAGASCAR · AUSTRALIA · ANTARCTICA

Our Solar System

SUN
Jupiter
Mercury
Venus
Earth
Mars
Asteroid belt
Saturn
Uranus

Titan
Rhea
Tethys
Mimas
Dione
Miranda
Saturn
Jupiter
Triton
Nereid
Pluto
Neptune
Uranus
Ganymede

	Pluto	Neptune	Uranus	Saturn	Jupiter
Diameter	1,485 mi (2,390 km)	30,775 mi (49,528 km)	31,763 mi (51,118 km)	74,897 mi (120,536 km)	88,846 mi (142,984 km)
Mean distance from Sun (millions of miles/millions of km)	3,647 mi (5,870 km)	2,793 mi (4,495 km)	1,785 mi (2,873 km)	891 mi (1,434 km)	484 mi (779 km)

Pluto

Neptune

	Approximate time to orbit the Sun	Average temperature
Sun	---	9,932°F (5,500°C)
Mercury	0.2 Earth year (88 days)	896°F (480°C)
Venus	0.6 Earth year (225 days)	626°F (330°C)
Earth	1 Earth year	72°F (22°C)
Mars	1.9 Earth years	-9°F (-23°C)
Jupiter	12 Earth years	-240°F (-151°C)
Saturn	29.5 Earth years	-300°F (-184°C)
Uranus	84 Earth years	-340°F (-206°C)
Neptune	165 Earth years	-370°F (-223°C)
Pluto	248 Earth years	-382°F (-230°C)

SUN

Callisto

Io Europa

Mars   Earth   Venus   Mercury

Moon

Phobos

Deimos

Note: Distances on the lower diagram are not shown to scale, and only major satellites are shown.

Mars	Earth	Venus	Mercury	Sun
4,222 mi (6,794 km)	7,926 mi (12,756 km)	7,521 mi (12,104 km)	3,032 mi (4,879 km)	863,706 mi (1,390,000 km)
142 mi (228 km)	93 mi (150 km)	67 mi (108 km)	36 mi (58 km)	-----

International boundary
▲ Mountain peak

North Polar Region

ARCTIC OCEAN

20°W 0° 20°E 40°E 60°E 80°E 100°E 120°E 140°E 160°E

Severnaya Zemlya
Greenland Sea
Norwegian Sea
Svalbard
Franz Josef Land
Novaya Zemlya
Kara Sea
Laptev Sea
East Siberian Sea
North Cape
ARCTIC CIRCLE 80°N
Iceland
Scandinavia
SIBERIA CENTRAL SIBERIAN PLATEAU VERKHOYANSK RANGE KOLYMA RANGE
60°N
Ireland British Isles North Sea NORTHERN EUROPEAN PLAIN Lake Ladoga Volga R. URAL MTS. WEST SIBERIAN PLAIN Ob R. Yenisey R. ASIA Lena R. Kamchatka Peninsula
EUROPE Mt. Elbrus 18,510 ft. (5,642 m) Lake Baikal Sea of Okhotsk
ALPS Danube R. Black Sea THE STEPPES Aral Sea KAZAKH UPLANDS ALTAY MTS. GOBI MANCHURIAN PLAIN Sakhalin Hokkaido 40°N
Iberian Peninsula Caspian Sea TIAN SHAN Taklimakan Desert NORTH CHINA PLAIN Sea of Japan Honshū
ATLAS MOUNTAINS Mediterranean Sea ZAGROS MTS. HINDU KUSH PLATEAU OF TIBET Mt. Everest 29,035 ft (8,850 m) Chang (Yangtze) R. Shikoku Kyūshū PACIFIC OCEAN
Canary Is. SAHARA Nile R. Red Sea Persian Gulf Mesopotamia HIMALAYAS East China Sea
Arabian Peninsula Thar Desert Ganges R. Taiwan TROPIC OF CANCER
AFRICA Rub' al-Khali DECCAN PLATEAU 20°N
SAHEL Arabian Sea Bay of Bengal Indochina Peninsula South China Sea Philippine Sea Philippine Islands Micronesia
ETHIOPIAN HIGHLANDS Cape Comorin Sri Lanka Malay Peninsula
Gulf of Guinea Somali Peninsula EQUATOR Melanesia 0°
Congo R. Lake Victoria Mt. Kilimanjaro 19,340 ft. (5,895 m) Borneo Sulawesi (Celebes) New Guinea Fiji Is.
CONGO BASIN Lake Tanganyika KATANGA PLATEAU Sumatra Java Cape York Pen. Coral Sea 20°S
Lake Malawi INDIAN OCEAN Great Sandy Desert GREAT DIVIDING RANGE New Caledonia
N W E S Kalahari Desert Madagascar WESTERN PLATEAU AUSTRALIA
ATLANTIC OCEAN TROPIC OF CAPRICORN Great Victoria Desert Mt. Kosciusko 7,310 ft. (2,228 m) Tasman Sea
Cape of Good Hope North Island 40°S
Kerguelen Is. Tasmania South Island
PRIME MERIDIAN
60°S
ANTARCTIC CIRCLE
Queen Maud Land Wilkes Land 80°S
ANTARCTICA
20°W 0° 20°E 40°E 60°E 80°E 100°E 120°E 140°E 160°E

South Polar Region

120°W 90°W PACIFIC OCEAN Cape Horn Drake Passage
Siple I. Thurston I. Amundsen Sea Bellingshausen Sea South Shetland Is.
180° Ross Sea ROCKEFELLER PLATEAU Marie Byrd Land Ellsworth Land Alexander I. Antarctic Peninsula 60°W
Scott Island Cape Adare Roosevelt I. Ross Ice Shelf ELLSWORTH MTS. Vinson Massif 16,067 ft. (4,897 m) Ronne Ice Shelf
Balleny Is. McMurdo Sound Ross I. QUEEN MAUD MTS. PENSACOLA MTS. Berkner I. Filchner Ice Shelf Weddell Sea South Orkney Is.
150°W PRINCE ALBERT MTS. TRANSANTARCTIC MOUNTAINS ANTARCTICA 30°W
South Pole Riiser-Larsen Ice Shelf ATLANTIC OCEAN
80°S Queen Maud Land Fimbul Ice Shelf
120°E Wilkes Land PRIME MERIDIAN
Cape Poinsett 70°S ANTARCTIC CIRCLE
60°E
AMERICAN HIGHLAND PRINCE CHARLES MTS. Enderby Land
Shackleton Ice Shelf Amery Ice Shelf Prydz Bay
90°E West Ice Shelf Davis Sea 0°
INDIAN OCEAN

0 500 1,000 mi
0 500 1,000 km

15

160°W 140°W 120°W 100°W 80°W 6

80°N

Alaska
(U.S.)

60°N

CANADA

**NORTH
AMERICA**

40°N

Azo
(Portu

UNITED STATES

Midway
Islands
(U.S.)

Bermuda
(U.K.)

ATLANTIC

Area of inset

OCEAN

TROPIC OF CANCER

20°N

Hawaii
(U.S.)

MEXICO

C
VE

PACIFIC

VENEZUELA **GUYANA** **SURINAME**

OCEAN

COLOMBIA French Guiana
(France)

0° EQUATOR

ECUADOR

Tokelau
(N.Z.) **KIRIBATI**

Galápagos
Islands
(Ecuador)

BRAZIL

**SOUTH
AMERICA**

PERU

American
SAMOA Samoa
(U.S.) Cook
Islands
(N.Z.)

French
Polynesia
(France)

BOLIVIA

PARAGUAY

20°S

TROPIC OF CAPRICORN

CHILE

TONGA Niue
(N.Z.)

Pitcairn Is.
(U.K.)

Easter Island
(Chile)

URUGUAY

ARGENTINA

Falkland
Islands
(U.K.)

40°S

PACIFIC

South
Georgia
(U.K.)

OCEAN

Central America and the Caribbean

100°W 90°W 80°W

UNITED STATES

30°N

60°S

ANTARCTIC CIRCLE

80°S

160°W 140°W 120°W 100°W 80°W

**ATLANTIC
OCEAN**

30°N
70°W

Gulf of Mexico

THE BAHAMAS

TROPIC OF CANCER

60°W

Turks and Caicos Is. (U.K.)

CUBA

Puerto
Rico
(U.S.) Anguilla (U.K.)

20°N

Cayman
Islands
(U.K.)

HAITI **DOMINICAN
REPUBLIC**

St. Martin **(Fr. and Neth.)**
ANTIGUA AND BARBUDA

MEXICO

JAMAICA

Virgin Islands
(U.S. and U.K.)

**ST. KITTS
AND NEVIS**

Montserrat (U.K.)
Guadeloupe (Fr.)
DOMINICA

BELIZE

Caribbean Sea

Martinique (Fr.)
ST. LUCIA

GUATEMALA **HONDURAS**

Aruba
(Neth.) Netherlands
Antilles
(Neth.)

BARBADOS
**ST. VINCENT AND
THE GRENADINES**

EL SALVADOR **NICARAGUA**

GRENADA **TRINIDAD AND
TOBAGO**

10°N

Panama
Canal

0 200 400 mi

10°N

**COSTA
RICA** **PANAMA**

0 200 400 km

**PACIFIC
OCEAN**

Projection: Azimuthal Equal-Area

90°W 80°W 70°W 60°W

International
boundary

Abbreviations

DEM. REP. CONGO	DEMOCRATIC REPUBLIC OF THE CONGO
EQ. GUINEA	EQUATORIAL GUINEA
NETH.	NETHERLANDS
N.Z.	NEW ZEALAND
REP. CONGO	REPUBLIC OF THE CONGO
U.A.E.	UNITED ARAB EMIRATES
U.K.	UNITED KINGDOM
U.S.	UNITED STATES

Europe

Ocean Floor

0   1,000   2,000 mi
0   1,000   2,000 km
Scale at the Equator
Projection: Mercator

ASIA

60°N

ALEUTIAN BASIN

ALEUTIAN TRENCH

NORTH AMERICA

KURIL TRENCH

NORTHWEST PACIFIC BASIN

30°N

PACIFIC BASIN

TROPIC OF CANCER

PHILIPPINE TRENCH

MARIANA TRENCH

-35,810 ft. (-10,915 m.)

0

EQUATOR

PACIFIC OCEAN

JAVA TRENCH

EAST PACIFIC RISE

TROPIC OF CAPRICORN

AUSTRALIA

30°S

KERMADEC TRENCH

SOUTHWEST PACIFIC BASIN

N

SOUTHEAST INDIAN RIDGE

SOUTH INDIAN BASIN

60°S

PACIFIC-ANTARCTIC RIDGE

SOUTHEAST PACIFIC BASIN

120°E

150°E

180

150°W

120°W

90°W

ANTARCTIC CIRCLE

ANTARCTICA

Surrounding most of the continents are gently sloping areas called continental shelves, which reach depths of about 650 ft. (200 m). At the edges of the continental shelves lie steeper continental slopes leading down to the deep ocean basin, or abyss. The abyss contains many of the same features we see on land, including plains, mountains ranges (ridges), isolated mountains (known as sea mounts or guyots), and trenches. The Mid-Ocean Ridge system marks the areas where crustal plates are moving apart, and is very active geologically, as molten rock rises and erupts to create new crust. Earthquakes and volcanoes are common along many undersea trenches and ridges.

Continent   Shoreline   Continental Shelf

Continental Slope

ARCTIC OCEAN

ARCTIC CIRCLE
NORWEGIAN BASIN

LABRADOR BASIN

60°N

EUROPE

ASIA

MID-ATLANTIC RIDGE

ATLANTIC OCEAN

30°N

AFRICA

ARABIAN BASIN

SOUTH AMERICA

PERU-CHILE TRENCH

MID-ATLANTIC RIDGE

ANGOLA BASIN

0°

INDIAN OCEAN

NINETYEAST RIDGE

WALVIS RIDGE

30°S

ARGENTINE BASIN

SOUTHWEST INDIAN RIDGE

KERGUELEN PLATEAU

ATLANTIC-INDIAN RIDGE

60°S

60°W | 30°W | 0° | 30°E | 60°E | 90°E

ANTARCTICA

Undersea Volcanoes | Mid-Ocean Ridge | Oceanic Trench | Continent

Abyssal Plain | Guyots

Plate Boundaries and Earthquakes

- Earthquake region
- • Location of major earthquake
- Plate boundary
- → Direction of plate movement

The movement of Earth's crustal plates causes the phenomena known as earthquakes. The surface of the Earth actually moves or quakes. An **earthquake** can have the destructive energy of an atomic bomb. However, thousands of earthquakes occur each day all over the world without most people realizing it.

The majority of earthquakes occur along a **fault.** A fault is usually a weak or broken area in the rocks beneath the surface of the Earth, but some, like the *San Andreas Fault* in California, can be seen on the surface. See pages 58–59 to learn more about faults.

The Richter Scale measures the energy of an earthquake. This measurement is obtained from the focus, or hypocenter, the spot where the first break in the rock layers occurs. The spot on the surface of the Earth, directly above the focus and nearest to the source of energy is called the epicenter.

Earthquake damage is caused by this energy, called seismic energy, moving through the rocks or along the surface. Many geographic factors, both physical and human, determine how much damage is done by these seismic waves of energy.

Major Earthquakes since 1900

Date	Location	Richter Scale Magnitude
April 4, 1905	Kangra, India	8.6
April 18, 1906	San Francisco, California	7.8
Dec. 28, 1908	Messina, Italy	7.5
Dec 16, 1920	Gansu Province, China	8.6
Sept. 1, 1923	Sagami Bay (near Yokohama), Japan	8.3
May 22, 1927	Xining, China	8.3
Dec. 25, 1932	Gansu Province, China	7.6
March 2, 1933	off northeast coast of Honshu, Japan	8.9
Jan. 15, 1934	Bihar, India/Nepal	8.4
May 30, 1935	Quetta, Pakistan	7.5
Jan. 25, 1939	Chillán, Chile	8.3
Dec. 26, 1939	Erzincan, Turkey	8.0
Dec. 21, 1946	Honshu, Japan	8.4
Oct. 5, 1948	Ashgabat, Turkmenistan	7.3
Aug. 15, 1950	Assam, India	8.7
May 22, 1960	Arauco, Chile	9.5
March 27, 1964	Anchorage, Alaska	9.2
May 31, 1970	Northern Peru, near Chimbote	7.8
Feb. 4, 1976	Guatemala City, Guatemala	7.5
July 28, 1976	Tangshan, China	8.0
Oct. 10, 1980	El Asnam, Algeria	7.7
Sept. 19, 1985	Mexico City, Mexico	8.1
June 20, 1990	Western Iran, near Qazvin	7.7
Dec. 12, 1992	Flores Island, Indonesia	7.5
Jan. 17, 1995	Kobe, Japan	6.9
Aug. 17, 1999	Istanbul, Turkey	7.4
Jan. 26, 2001	Ahmadabad, India	7.7

Source: National Earthquake Information Center, U.S.G.S

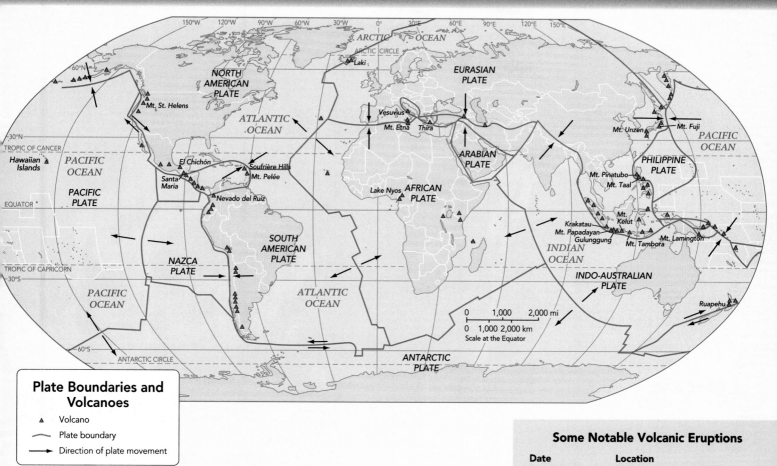

Plate Boundaries and Volcanoes

▲ Volcano

⌒ Plate boundary

→ Direction of plate movement

A **volcano** is an opening in the Earth's crust often capped by a cone-shaped hill or mountain formed from erupted lava and ash.

Volcanoes are associated with plate boundaries. Powerful forces occurring far beneath the surface at the edges of plates cause rock to melt and, at the same time, open cracks in the crust. An eruption occurs when magma (melted rock) flows, and many times explodes, through a weakness, such as a crack in the Earth's crust. Once magma is flowing on the Earth's surface it is called lava. Flowing lava can be several thousand degrees Fahrenheit.

In a few cases, volcanoes exist without being near the edge of a plate. In these cases, such as the Hawaiian Islands, a powerful and persistent flow of magma has broken through the crust.

Some Notable Volcanic Eruptions

Date	Location
1500 B.C.	Thira (Santorini), Greece
Aug. 24, A.D. 79	Vesuvius, Italy
1169	Mt. Etna, Italy
1586	Mt. Kelut, Java, Indonesia
Dec. 15, 1631	Vesuvius, Italy
March–July, 1669	Mt. Etna, Italy
Aug. 12, 1772	Mt. Papandayan, Java, Indonesia
June 8, 1783	Laki, Iceland
May 21, 1792	Mt. Unzen, Japan
Apr. 10–12, 1815	Mt. Tambora, Sumbawa, Indonesia
Oct. 8, 1822	Galunggung, Java, Indonesia
Aug. 26–28, 1883	Krakatau, Indonesia
Apr. 24, 1902	Santa Maria, Guatemala
May 8, 1902	Mt. Pelée, Martinique
Jan. 30, 1911	Mt. Taal, Philippines
May 19, 1919	Mt. Kelut, Java, Indonesia
Jan. 17–21, 1951	Mt. Lamington, New Guinea
May 18, 1980	Mt. St. Helens, United States
Mar. 28, 1982	El Chichon, Mexico
Nov. 13, 1985	Nevado del Ruiz, Colombia
Aug. 21, 1986	Lake Nyos, Cameroon
June 15, 1991	Mt. Pinatubo, Philippines
June–Sept., 1997	Soufrière Hills, Montserrat

Crater

Branch Pipe

Buried Dome

Lava Flow

Fissure Flows

Pyroclastic Layers

Sill

Magma Chamber

237 Million Years Ago

SIBERIA

ASIA

URAL MOUNTAINS

Greenland

EUROPE

PALEO-TETHYS OCEAN

NORTH AMERICA

SPAIN   ITALY

CHINA

TURKEY

PANGEA

IRAN

TIBET

AFRICA

ARABIA

TETHYS OCEAN

PANTHALASSIC OCEAN

SOUTH AMERICA

MADAGASCAR

NEW GUINEA

ANDES MOUNTAINS

INDIA

AUSTRALIA

GONDWANA

ANTARCTICA

This peculiar—to our eyes—arrangement of continents with its unfamiliar oceans and seas, mountains and plains, and peninsulas and islands reminds us that the dinosaurs lived in a far different landscape than our own. As the last dinosaurs receded into memory, the future Atlantic Ocean and Mediterranean Sea were becoming more substantial and recognizable, and the continents, except for Australia and Antarctica, were nearing their present latitudes. Within the last 65 million years, most continents nestled unhurriedly into their current positions. However, the Indian sub-continent "sprinted" north, crashing into Asia and bulldozing up the Himalayas, earth's loftiest mountain range.

237   **94**   **65**

Age of Dinosaurs

300   250   200   150   100

Millions of Years Ago

DECEMBER						
1	2	3	4	5	6	7
8	9	10	11	12	13	14
15	16	17	18	19	20	21
22	23	24	25	26	27	28
29	30	31	JANUARY			

NOVEMBER

OCTOBER

SEPTEMBER

94 Million Years Ago

The highly controversial theory of Continental Drift was proposed in 1915 by Alfred Wegener to explain both geologic and fossil discoveries. Although supported by strong data and seemingly obvious visual evidence—most notably, the close fit of the coastlines of Africa and South America—the theory was rejected by other scientists. By the 1960s, further studies, especially those that discovered that some rocks contained a record of the alignment of the Earth's magnetic field, resurrected the theory, which was redefined under the term Plate Tectonics. Few scientists now dispute its general premise, that continental and oceanic plates move atop a layer of hot and semi-solid rock below them, although many details, particularly the causes and mechanics of the motion, are still not well understood.

65 Million Years Ago

Present day

Humans

Present Day

If a year (365 days) represented the approximate age of the Earth (4.5 billion years), then the first map which shows the Earth 237 million years ago, would have occurred about December 13th. 94 and 65 million years ago would have occurred about December 25th and 27th respectively.

Recorded history started about 5,500 years ago: on this calendar, that would have been about 21 seconds before the New Year.

Climate

- Tropical wet
- Tropical wet and dry
- Arid
- Semiarid
- Mediterranean
- Humid subtropical
- Marine
- Humid continental
- Subarctic
- Tundra
- Ice cap
- Highland

- Highest average annual precipitation
- Lowest average annual preciptation
- Highest recorded temperature
- Lowest recorded temperature

Major Ocean Currents
- Cool currents
- Warm currents

NORTH AMERICA

SOUTH AMERICA

ATLANTIC OCEAN

PACIFIC OCEAN

Fairbanks
Iqaluit
Nuuk
Edmonton
Vancouver
Toronto
St. John's
Chicago
Denver
New York City
San Francisco
Phoenix
Atlanta
Miami
Mexico City
San Juan
Caracas
Bogotá
Lima
Recife
Arica 0.03" (0.08 cm)
São Paulo
Rio de Janeiro
Santiago
Buenos Aires
Punta Arenas

80°N
60°N
40°N
TROPIC OF CANCER
20°N
0° EQUATOR
20°S
TROPIC OF CAPRICORN
40°S
60°S
ANTARCTIC CIRCLE
80°S

160°W 140°W 120°W 100°W 80°W 60°W

Arid

Highland

Humid continental

Icecap

Marine

Mediterranean

Semiarid

ARCTIC OCEAN

ARCTIC CIRCLE

Reykjavík

Tromsø
Murmansk

Stockholm
London
EUROPE
Paris
Rome
Istanbul

Casablanca
El Azizia 136°F
(58°C)
Cairo

AFRICA
Lagos
Addis Ababa

Kinshasa
Nairobi

Dakar

Moscow

Novosibirsk

Yakutsk

ASIA

Beijing
Seoul
Tokyo

Tehran
Kabul

Baghdad
Riyadh
Karachi
New Delhi

Shanghai

Mawsynram 467" (1,186 cm)

Kolkata
(Calcutta)
Hong Kong

Mumbai
(Bombay)

Bangkok
Manila

Ho Chi Minh
City

Jakarta

PACIFIC OCEAN

TROPIC OF CANCER

INDIAN OCEAN

AUSTRALIA

TROPIC OF CAPRICORN

Johannesburg

Brisbane

Perth
Sydney
Melbourne
Auckland

Cape
Town

N
W E
S

0   1,000   2,000 mi
0   1,000   2,000 km
Scale at the Equator
Projection: Robinson

ANTARCTICA

Vostok −129°F (−89°C)

80°S

Humid subtropical

Subarctic

Tropical wet

Tropical wet and dry

Tundra

Vegetation

- Unclassified highlands or ice cap
- Tundra and alpine tundra
- Coniferous forest
- Midlatitude deciduous forest
- Subtropical broadleaf evergreen forest
- Mixed forest
- Midlatitude scrubland
- Midlatitude grassland
- Desert
- Tropical seasonal and scrub
- Tropical rain forest
- Tropical savanna

160°W 140°W 120°W 100°W 80°W 60°W
80°N
60°N

Fairbanks
Iqaluit
Nuuk

Edmonton
Vancouver
NORTH AMERICA
Toronto
St. John's

40°N
Denver
Chicago
New York City
San Francisco
Phoenix
Atlanta
ATLANTIC OCEAN

Miami

TROPIC OF CANCER
20°N
Mexico City
San Juan

PACIFIC OCEAN

Caracas
Bogotá

0° EQUATOR

SOUTH AMERICA
Lima
Recife

20°S
TROPIC OF CAPRICORN
São Paulo
Rio de Janeiro

Santiago
Buenos Aires

40°S

PACIFIC OCEAN

60°S
Punta Arenas

ANTARCTIC CIRCLE
80°S
160°W 140°W 120°W 100°W 80°W 60°W

Coniferous forest

Deciduous forest

Desert

Midlatitude scrubland

Mixed forest

Subtropical broadleaf evergreen forest

Tropical rain forest

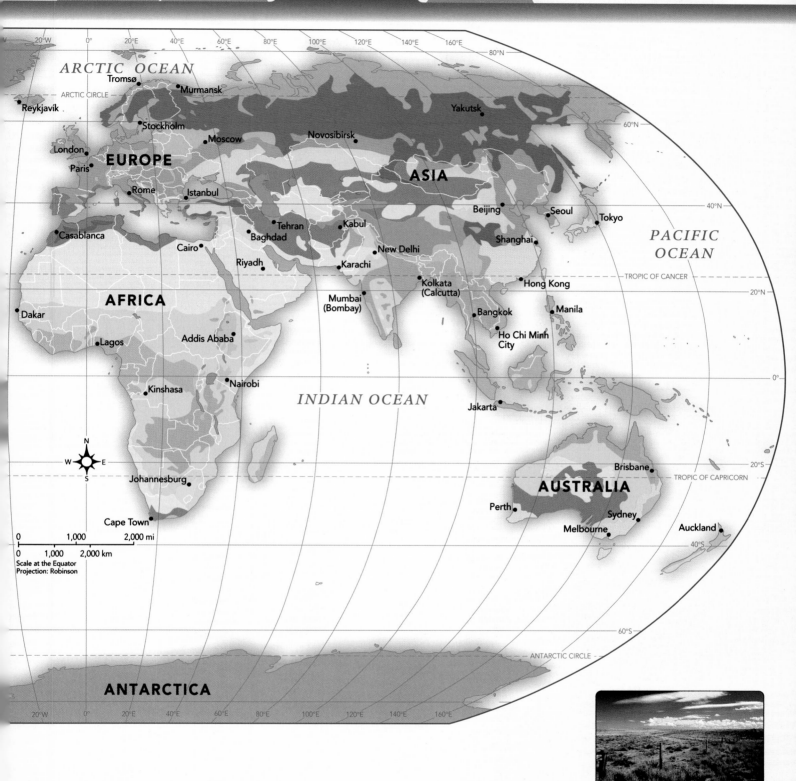

ARCTIC OCEAN

Tromsø
Murmansk
ARCTIC CIRCLE
Reykjavík
Yakutsk
Stockholm
60°N
London
Moscow
Novosibirsk
EUROPE
ASIA
Paris
40°N
Rome
Istanbul
Beijing
Seoul
Tokyo
Tehran
Kabul
Shanghai
PACIFIC OCEAN
Casablanca
Baghdad
New Delhi
Cairo
Karachi
Hong Kong
TROPIC OF CANCER
Riyadh
Kolkata (Calcutta)
20°N
AFRICA
Mumbai (Bombay)
Bangkok
Manila
Dakar
Ho Chi Minh City
Lagos
Addis Ababa
0°
Kinshasa
Nairobi
Jakarta
INDIAN OCEAN
N
W E
S
AUSTRALIA
20°S
Johannesburg
Brisbane
TROPIC OF CAPRICORN
Perth
Sydney
Cape Town
Melbourne
Auckland
0   1,000   2,000 mi
0   1,000   2,000 km
40°S
Scale at the Equator
Projection: Robinson

ANTARCTICA

ANTARCTIC CIRCLE

60°S

Midlatitude grassland

Tropical savanna

Tropical seasonal and scrub

Tundra and alpine tundra

Unclassified highlands or ice cap

World Forest Cover

Forests help regulate climate by storing huge amounts of carbon dioxide, while providing habitats for countless animal and plant species. Environmentalists have voiced concern over a long-term decrease in forest cover, as forest lands have been cleared for such purposes as farming, logging, mining, and urban expansion.

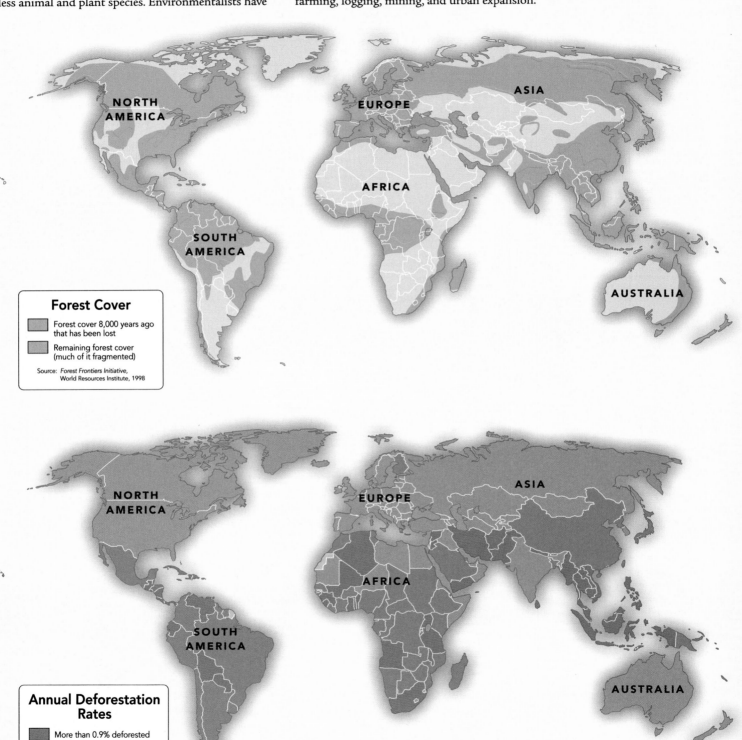

Forest Cover

Forest cover 8,000 years ago that has been lost

Remaining forest cover (much of it fragmented)

Source: *Forest Frontiers Initiative, World Resources Institute, 1998*

Annual Deforestation Rates

More than 0.9% deforested

0.1 to 0.9% deforested

Stable or increased forest area

No current data available

Source: World Resources Institute

Tropical Rain Forests

Tropical rain forests, found around the Earth within 10 degrees of the equator, contain more than half of all the world's plants and animal species, besides to being home to many indigenous peoples. They are vital to the balance of nature. In the past 40 years alone, about one-fifth of the acreage has been cleared for logging and other purposes. These rain forests, including the major forests pinpointed here, remain under serious threat.

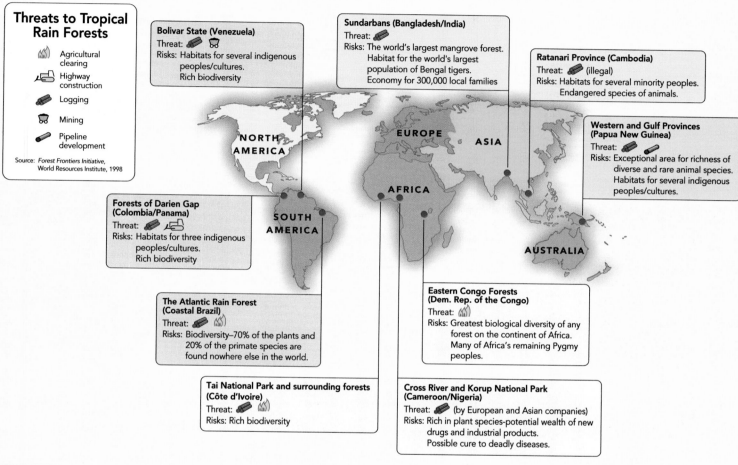

Threats to Tropical Rain Forests

- Agricultural clearing
- Highway construction
- Logging
- Mining
- Pipeline development

Source: *Forest Frontiers Initiative, World Resources Institute, 1998*

Bolivar State (Venezuela)
Threat:
Risks: Habitats for several indigenous peoples/cultures. Rich biodiversity

Sundarbans (Bangladesh/India)
Threat:
Risks: The world's largest mangrove forest. Habitat for the world's largest population of Bengal tigers. Economy for 300,000 local families

Ratanari Province (Cambodia)
Threat: (illegal)
Risks: Habitats for several minority peoples. Endangered species of animals.

Western and Gulf Provinces (Papua New Guinea)
Threat:
Risks: Exceptional area for richness of diverse and rare animal species. Habitats for several indigenous peoples/cultures.

Forests of Darien Gap (Colombia/Panama)
Threat:
Risks: Habitats for three indigenous peoples/cultures. Rich biodiversity

The Atlantic Rain Forest (Coastal Brazil)
Threat:
Risks: Biodiversity–70% of the plants and 20% of the primate species are found nowhere else in the world.

Eastern Congo Forests (Dem. Rep. of the Congo)
Threat:
Risks: Greatest biological diversity of any forest on the continent of Africa. Many of Africa's remaining Pygmy peoples.

Tai National Park and surrounding forests (Côte d'Ivoire)
Threat:
Risks: Rich biodiversity

Cross River and Korup National Park (Cameroon/Nigeria)
Threat: (by European and Asian companies)
Risks: Rich in plant species-potential wealth of new drugs and industrial products. Possible cure to deadly diseases.

NORTH AMERICA · SOUTH AMERICA · EUROPE · AFRICA · ASIA · AUSTRALIA

Percentage of Frontier Forest Under Moderate or High Threat of Destruction
(through 2030)

Source: *Forest Frontiers Initiative, World Resources Institute, 1998*

According to the World Resources Institute, only about one-fifth of the Earth's forest cover of 8,000 years ago survives unfragmented, in the large unspoiled tracts it calls *frontier forests*. These forests are big enough to provide stable habitats for a rich diversity of plant and animal species.

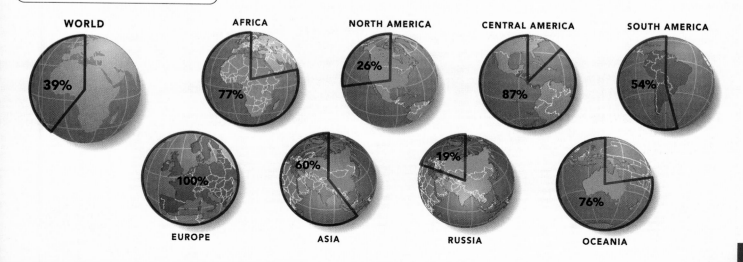

WORLD 39%
AFRICA 77%
NORTH AMERICA 26%
CENTRAL AMERICA 87%
SOUTH AMERICA 54%
EUROPE 100%
ASIA 60%
RUSSIA 19%
OCEANIA 76%

Population

Population
Issues

Languages/
Literacy/Religions

Land Use/GDP/
Employment

Mining/Energy

Population Density 2002

Persons per sq. mile	Persons per sq. km
Over 520	Over 200
260 to 519	100 to 199
130 to 259	50 to 99
25 to 129	10 to 49
1 to 24	1 to 9
0	0

● Urban agglomerations with over 10,000,000 inhabitants

World population total as of March 1, 2003: 6,277,603,768
(Every day it increases by about 202,500)

Source: International Programs Center, U.S. Bureau of the Census

Largest Cities (urban agglomerations)

	2000		2015 (projected)
1	Tokyo 26,444,000	1	Tokyo 26,444,000
2	Mexico City 18,131,000	2	Mumbai 26,138,000
3	Mumbai 18,066,000	3	Lagos 23,173,000
4	São Paulo 17,755,000	4	Dhaka 21,119,000
5	New York 16,640,000	5	São Paulo 20,397,000
6	Lagos 13,427,000	6	Karachi 19,211,000
7	Los Angeles 13,140,000	7	Mexico City 19,180,000
8	Kolkata 12,918,000	8	New York 17,432,000
9	Shanghai. 12,887,000	9	Jakarta 17,256,000
10	Buenos Aires . . . 12,560,000	10	Kolkata 17,252,000
11	Dhaka 12,317,000	11	Delhi 16,808,000
12	Karachi 11,794,000	12	Manila. 14,825,000
13	Delhi 11,695,000	13	Shanghai. 14,575,000
14	Jakarta 11,018,000	14	Los Angeles 14,080,000
15	Osaka. 11,013,000	15	Buenos Aires . . . 14,076,000

Source: United Nations Population Division

Population Projections by Continent

YEAR 2000 2025 2050

Source: U.S. Bureau of the Census, International Data Division

New York City

Los Angeles

Mexico City

São Paulo

Rio de Janeiro

Buenos Aires

NORTH AMERICA
480,545,000
617,249,000
728,136,000

EUROPE*
588,240,000
696,838,000
728,982,000

ASIA
3,688,072,000
4,774,053,000
5,406,328,000

AFRICA
2,012,567,000
1,317,493,000
805,243,000

SOUTH AMERICA
346,504,000
451,641,000
519,878,000

AUSTRALIA & PACIFIC IS.
30,795,000
38,512,000
42,829,000

ARCTIC OCEAN

PACIFIC OCEAN

ATLANTIC OCEAN

INDIAN OCEAN

Equator

ATLANTIC OCEAN

*Including Russia

Population Density by Country

The world will become more crowded in the 21st century. In mid-2000, China already had the highest population in the world, with an estimated 1.3 billion inhabitants, one-fifth of the world total. India had reached 1 billion, while the United States had the world's third-largest population, with about 275 million, followed by Indonesia, Brazil, and Russia.

Persons per sq. mile	Persons per sq. km
1170 and over	450 and over
780 to 1169	300 to 449
390 to 779	150 to 299
195 to 389	75 to 149
65 to 194	25 to 74
Under 65	Under 25
	Other countries

Source: U.S. Bureau of the Census, U.S. Dept. of Commerce

Population Density of the Current Most Populous Countries

2000	Persons per square mile	2050 (projected)	Persons per square mile
China	330	China	360
India	800	India	1,450
United States	70	United States	100
Indonesia	290	Indonesia	450
Brazil	50	Brazil	70
Russia	20	Russia	20

2000

UNITED STATES

BRAZIL

RUSSIA

CHINA

INDIA

INDONESIA

2050

UNITED STATES

BRAZIL

RUSSIA

CHINA

INDIA

INDONESIA

Life Expectancy

Life expectancy at birth is a common measure of the number of years a person may expect to live. There are many factors, such as nutrition, sanitation, health and medical services, that contribute to helping people live longer.

As some of the above factors improve in the develop-ing countries, life expectancy there should increase. But most of sub-Saharan Africa will have less than average life expectancies.

Although it is not included here, females almost always have a longer life expectancy than males.

2000

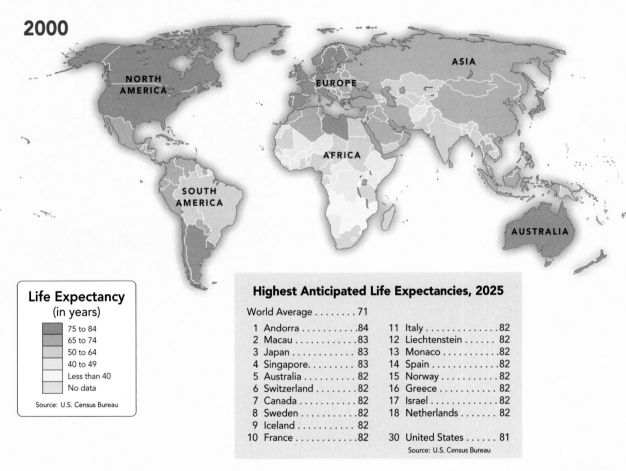

Life Expectancy
(in years)

- 75 to 84
- 65 to 74
- 50 to 64
- 40 to 49
- Less than 40
- No data

Source: U.S. Census Bureau

Highest Anticipated Life Expectancies, 2025

World Average 71

#	Country		#	Country	
1	Andorra	84	11	Italy	82
2	Macau	83	12	Liechtenstein	82
3	Japan	83	13	Monaco	82
4	Singapore	83	14	Spain	82
5	Australia	82	15	Norway	82
6	Switzerland	82	16	Greece	82
7	Canada	82	17	Israel	82
8	Sweden	82	18	Netherlands	82
9	Iceland	82			
10	France	82	30	United States	81

Source: U.S. Census Bureau

2025

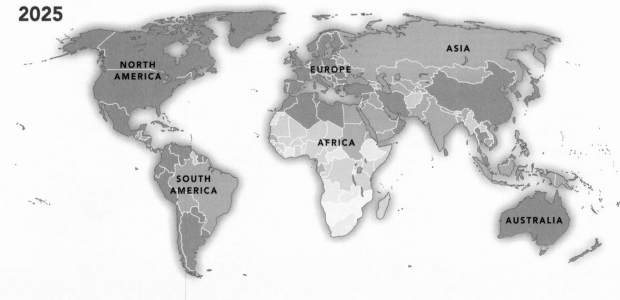

Youthful Population

A country with a youthful population often reflects a high birthrate and a short life expectancy. The youthful component of a country's population should be the healthiest and the most energetic. In countries where there is a good system of education, the standards of living can only benefit from a large, educated youthful population. Furthermore, large numbers of young workers offer a means for providing financial and social support for the older members of the population. Unfortunately, a country's economic and physical resources may not be able to absorb a ballooning youthful population. A lack of opportunity in rural regions encourages migration to over-crowded cities where, in turn, a lack of jobs or space in schools leads to swelling numbers of unemployed.

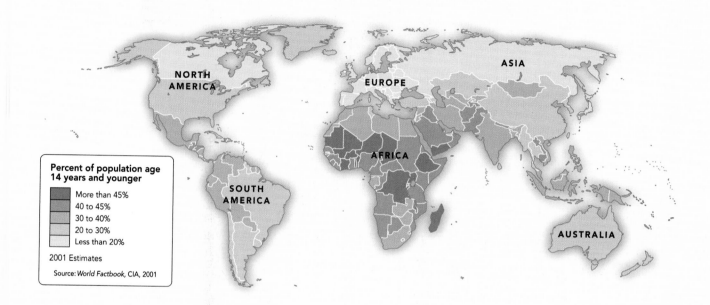

Percent of population age 14 years and younger

- More than 45%
- 40 to 45%
- 30 to 40%
- 20 to 30%
- Less than 20%

2001 Estimates

Source: *World Factbook*, CIA, 2001

Food and Nutrition

There has been a general trend towards better nutrition, but sub-Saharan Africa remains a problem area: increasing numbers of people will be suffering from undernutrition.

On a worldwide basis, the food supply seems adequate. Unfortunately the availability of food and the distribution of people don't always match up.

UNITED STATES 3,772
HAITI 2,056
BOLIVIA 2,218
ARGENTINA 3,181
AUSTRIA 3,757
BULGARIA 2,467
ISRAEL 3,562
AFGHANISTAN 1,539
EGYPT 3,346
DEMOCRATIC REPUBLIC OF THE CONGO 1,514
PAPUA NEW GUINEA 2,175
NEW ZEALAND 3,252

Average Daily per Capita Calorie Supply, 1998–2000

Within each continent, the countries with the highest per capita calorie supply are labeled in green, while the countries with the lowest per capital calorie supply are labeled in red.

Source: UN Food and Agriculture Organization

Undernutrition in Developing Countries, 1969–2010

Millions of persons suffering from undernutrition

NEAR EAST & NORTH AFRICA
LATIN AMERICA
SUB-SAHARAN AFRICA
SOUTH ASIA
EAST & SOUTHEAST ASIA

The colors of the regions correspond to the colors in the graph.

Languages / Literacy / Religions

Top map (Languages):

English
Inuktitut
Inuit
Inuit
English
Cree
French
English
NORTH AMERICA
English
Icelandic
Norwegian
Swedish
Finnish
English
EUROPE
German
Ukranian
Russian
Russian
Yakut
Chukchi
French
Hungarian
ASIA
Russian
Kazakh
Mongolian
Georgian
Uzbek
Turkic
Portuguese
Spanish
Italian
Greek
Turkish
Turkmenian
Chinese (Mandarin)
Korean
Arabic
Hebrew
Kurdish
Arabic
Farsi
Pashto
Tibetan
Japanese
Arabic
Punjabi
Chinese (many dialects)
Spanish
French
Spanish
Spanish
English
French
Arabic
Hindi
Bengali
Burmese
Thai
Vietnam-ese
Tamil
Tagalog (Pilipino)
English, Hawaiian
Spanish
Quechua
Spanish
SOUTH AMERICA
Portuguese
Fulani
Bambara
Hausa
Fulani
Akan
Yoruba
Igbo
AFRICA
Amharic
Somali
Gikuyu
Swahili
Luba Lulua
Kongo
Rwanda
Makua
Shona
Malagasy
Sinhalese
Malay
Malay
Javanese
Papuan (many dialects)
Afrikaans, English
Zulu
Xhosa
AUSTRALIA
English
English

Languages

- African (including Yoruba, Swahili)
- Afro-Asiatic (including Hebrew, Arabic)
- Amerindian (including Inuit, Iroquoian, Quechua)
- Dravidian
- Indo-European (including English, Spanish, Hindi)
- Japanese and Korean
- Malayo-Polynesian (including Hawaiian, Pilipino)
- Sino-Tibetan (including Chinese, Burmese)
- Ural-Asiatic (including Finnish, Hungarian, Turkish)
- Other
- Uninhabited

French   Primary regional language

Bottom map (Literacy):

NORTH AMERICA
SOUTH AMERICA
EUROPE
ASIA
AFRICA
AUSTRALIA

Literacy

2001 Estimates

- 97 to 100%
- 81 to 96%
- 61 to 80%
- 30 to 60%
- Less than 30%
- No current data available

World literacy rates are based on the percentage of the population who can read their native language. The data varies between the years of 1989 to 2000.

Source: *World Factbook*, CIA, 2001

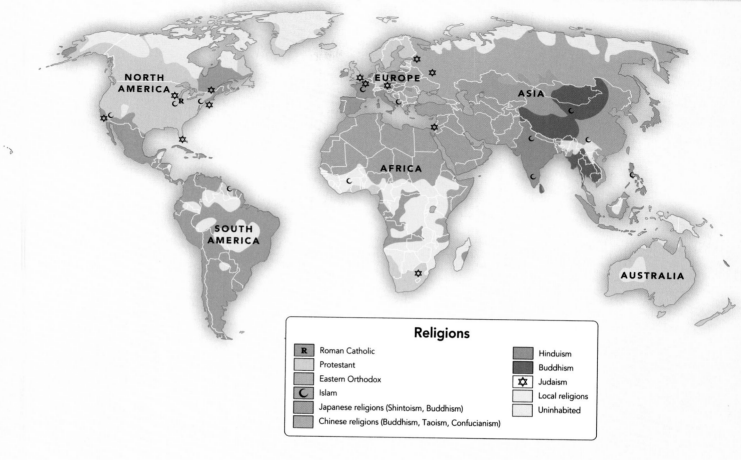

Religions

R	Roman Catholic		Hinduism
	Protestant		Buddhism
	Eastern Orthodox	✡	Judaism
☪	Islam		Local religions
	Japanese religions (Shintoism, Buddhism)		Uninhabited
	Chinese religions (Buddhism, Taoism, Confucianism)		

Historical Spread of Religions

- Buddhism
- Christianity
- Hinduism
- Islam
- Judaism (Jewish diaspora)
- Present-day boundaries

Land Use

- Commercial agriculture
- Dairying
- Livestock ranching
- Nomadic herding
- Subsistence agriculture
- Primarily forestland
- Limited agricultural activity
- ● Major manufacturing and trade centers

Shares of the World's GDP 2001

Source: *World Factbook*, CIA, 2001

Canada 2%

Japan 7%

European Union 19%

Rest of the world 49%

United States 23%

The Gross Domestic Product (GDP) is the value of goods and services produced by a political entity in any given period. These values help indicate how well the economy is doing.

150°W   120°W   90°W   60°W

60°N

NORTH AMERICA

Seattle/Tacoma

Detroit   Toronto
Chicago   Boston
St Louis   New York City
          Philadelphia

San Francisco/San Jose

Los Angeles

Charlotte

ATLANTIC OCEAN

30°N

Houston

TROPIC OF CANCER

PACIFIC OCEAN

Mexico City/ Puebla

Caracas

EQUATOR

0°

SOUTH AMERICA

Belo Horizonte

Rio de Janeiro

São Paulo

TROPIC OF CAPRICORN

Santiago/Valparaíso

Buenos Aires

30°S

60°S

ANTARCTIC CIRCLE

150°W   120°W   90°W   60°W

Industrial Employment

- More than 40%
- 30 to 40%
- 15 to 29.9%
- Less than 15%
- No current data available

Percentage of total labor force employed in industry.

Source: *World Factbook*, CIA, 2001

ARCTIC OCEAN

ARCTIC CIRCLE

Stockholm
London
Birmingham
Brussels
Paris
Marseille
Barcelona
Amsterdam/
Rotterdam
Colonge/Essen
Milan/Turin

St. Petersburg
Moscow
Katowice/
Krakow
Donetsk

EUROPE

Yekaterinburg

Novosibirsk

60°N

Tashkent

ASIA

Shenyang
Beijing/
Tianjin
Wuhan

Seoul
Shanghai
Taipei
Hong
Kong

Tokyo/Yokohama
Osaka/
Kobe

PACIFIC
OCEAN

30°N

TROPIC OF CANCER

AFRICA

Mumbai
(Bombay)

Kolkata
(Calcutta)

Singapore

INDIAN
OCEAN

Jakarta

0°

Johannesburg-
Pretoria

TROPIC OF CAPRICORN

AUSTRALIA

30°S

N
W   E
S

Cape Town

Sydney
Melbourne

0   1,000   2,000 mi

0   1,000   2,000 km
Scale at the Equator
Projection: Robinson

60°S

ANTARCTIC CIRCLE

ANTARCTICA

Agricultural Employment

	More than 80%
	60 to 80%
	30 to 59.9%
	10 to 29.9%
	Less than 10%
	No current data available

Percent of total labor force
employed in agriculture.

Source: *World Factbook*, CIA, 2001

Oil, Natural Gas, and Coal

- Major oil fields
- Other oil fields
- Natural gas fields
- Coal deposits

Major Minerals

- Al Bauxite
- Cr Chromium
- Cu Copper
- Diamonds
- Au Gold
- Fe Iron
- Pb Lead
- Mn Manganese
- Ni Nickel
- Pt Platinum
- Ag Silver
- Sn Tin
- Ti Titanium
- Zn Zinc

Scale at the Equator
Projection: Robinson

PACIFIC
OCEAN

AUSTRALIA

Electrical Energy Production

Billions of kilowatt hours, 1999

- 3,705 (United States)
- 500 to 1,175
- 100 to 499
- 50 to 99
- 20 to 49
- Less than 20
- No current data available

Source: U.S. Department of Energy,
International Energy Annual, 2000

ASIA

PACIFIC
OCEAN

INDIAN
OCEAN

AUSTRALIA

Energy Consumption

- United States
- Rest of world

Energy consumption (quadrillion Btu)

Population (billions)

Petroleum   Coal   Natural gas   Hydro-electric   Nuclear   Geothermal, wind, solar & biomass

Source: U.S. Department of Energy, *International Energy Annual, 2000*

Despite having only about 4.6% of the world's population, the United States consumes a disproportionate amount of the world's energy.

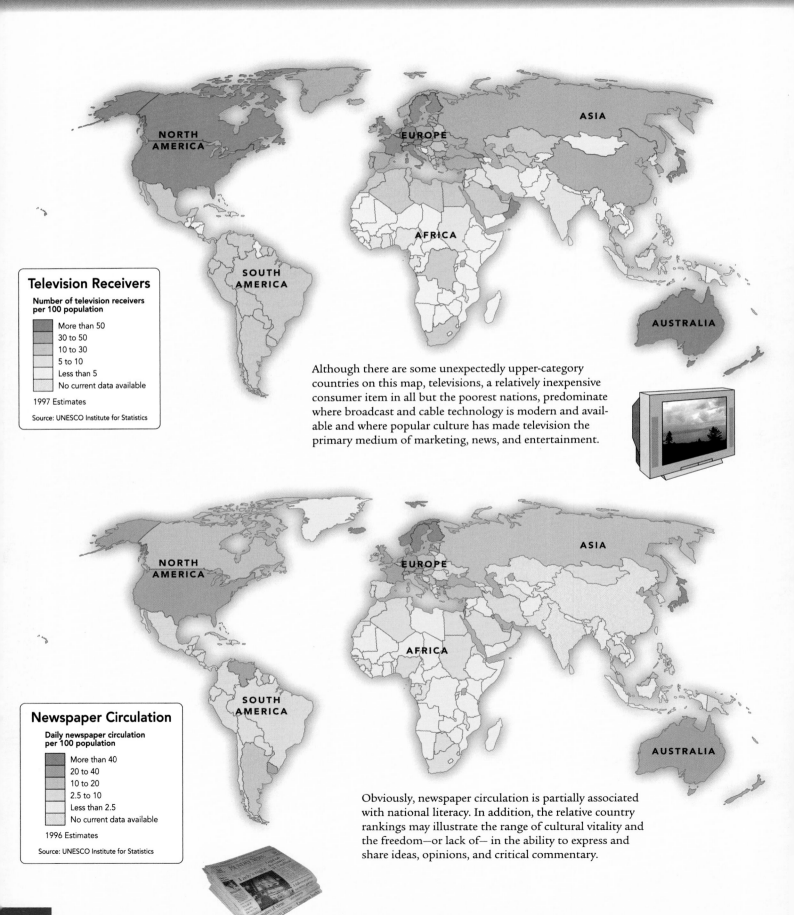

Television Receivers

Number of television receivers per 100 population

- More than 50
- 30 to 50
- 10 to 30
- 5 to 10
- Less than 5
- No current data available

1997 Estimates

Source: UNESCO Institute for Statistics

Although there are some unexpectedly upper-category countries on this map, televisions, a relatively inexpensive consumer item in all but the poorest nations, predominate where broadcast and cable technology is modern and available and where popular culture has made television the primary medium of marketing, news, and entertainment.

Newspaper Circulation

Daily newspaper circulation per 100 population

- More than 40
- 20 to 40
- 10 to 20
- 2.5 to 10
- Less than 2.5
- No current data available

1996 Estimates

Source: UNESCO Institute for Statistics

Obviously, newspaper circulation is partially associated with national literacy. In addition, the relative country rankings may illustrate the range of cultural vitality and the freedom—or lack of— in the ability to express and share ideas, opinions, and critical commentary.

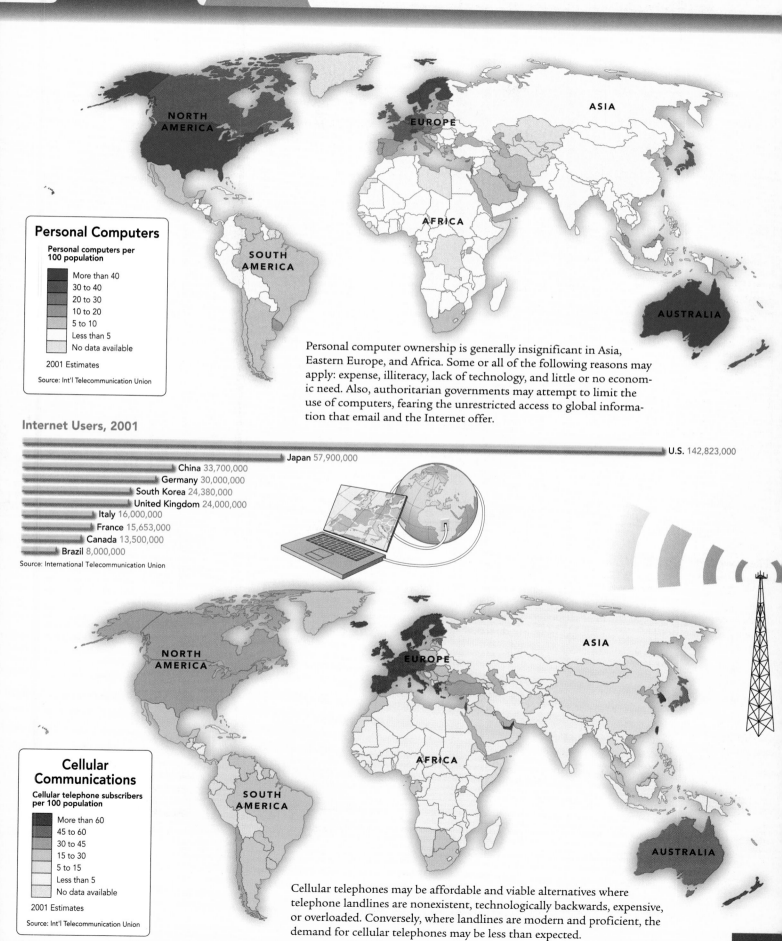

Personal Computers

Personal computers per 100 population

- More than 40
- 30 to 40
- 20 to 30
- 10 to 20
- 5 to 10
- Less than 5
- No data available

2001 Estimates

Source: Int'l Telecommunication Union

Personal computer ownership is generally insignificant in Asia, Eastern Europe, and Africa. Some or all of the following reasons may apply: expense, illiteracy, lack of technology, and little or no economic need. Also, authoritarian governments may attempt to limit the use of computers, fearing the unrestricted access to global information that email and the Internet offer.

Internet Users, 2001

- U.S. 142,823,000
- Japan 57,900,000
- China 33,700,000
- Germany 30,000,000
- South Korea 24,380,000
- United Kingdom 24,000,000
- Italy 16,000,000
- France 15,653,000
- Canada 13,500,000
- Brazil 8,000,000

Source: International Telecommunication Union

Cellular Communications

Cellular telephone subscribers per 100 population

- More than 60
- 45 to 60
- 30 to 45
- 15 to 30
- 5 to 15
- Less than 5
- No data available

2001 Estimates

Source: Int'l Telecommunication Union

Cellular telephones may be affordable and viable alternatives where telephone landlines are nonexistent, technologically backwards, expensive, or overloaded. Conversely, where landlines are modern and proficient, the demand for cellular telephones may be less than expected.

Time Zones

Non-standard time

| 11 P.M. | Mid-night | 1 A.M. | 2 A.M. | 3 A.M. | 4 A.M. | 5 A.M. | 6 A.M. | 7 A.M. | 8 A.M. | 9 A.M. | 10 A.M. | 11 A.M. | Noon | 1 P.M. | 2 P.M. | 3 P.M. | 4 P.M. | 5 P.M. | 6 P.M. | 7 P.M. | 8 P.M. | 9 P.M. | 10 P.M |

Prime Meridian

International Date Line

NORTH AMERICA

Anchorage

San Francisco
Los Angeles

Chicago
Montreal
Washington, D.C.

Mexico City

-4

0

-3½

Dublin
Paris

Moscow

EUROPE

ASIA

Cairo

AFRICA

Beijing

CHINA

+3½ +4½ +5²/₃

Delhi
+5½

+6½

+5½

+6

+6½

Lima

SOUTH AMERICA

Buenos Aires

+12

-9½

-8½

Johannesburg

AUSTRALIA
+9½

Sydne

+11½

+13

+10½

+12¾

Hours

| +11 | +12 -12 | -11 | -10 | -9 | -8 | -7 | -6 | -5 | -4 | -3 | -2 | -1 | 0 | +1 | +2 | +3 | +4 | +5 | +6 | +7 | +8 | +9 | +10 |

The World is divided into 24 time zones, beginning at the Prime Meridian, which runs through Greenwich, England. The twelve zones east and twelve zones west of the Prime Meridian meet halfway around the globe at the International Date Line.

Traveling in an easterly direction, the time of day moves ahead one hour for each zone crossed. Traveling west, time falls behind one hour per zone. At the International Date Line a traveler gains one day crossing it in an easterly direction, and loses one day traveling west.

Note that the times shown are "standard time." Adjustments are necessary when "daylight saving time" is used.

Average Speeds of
Some Passenger Transportation

Walking 3–4 mph/5-6 kph

Bicycle 10 mph/16 kph

Ocean liner, *Queen Elizabeth II* 33 mph/53 kph

Intercity bus, Greyhound; U.S. 54 mph/87 kph

Air cushion vehicle, United Kingdom 69 mph/111kph

Electric train, Amtrak *Acela Express*; Eastern U.S. 150 mph/241 kph (top speed)

High-speed train, *Shinkansen* (Bullet Train); Japan 164 mph/263 kph (average speed between stations)

Jet airliner, Boeing 737 500 mph/805 kph

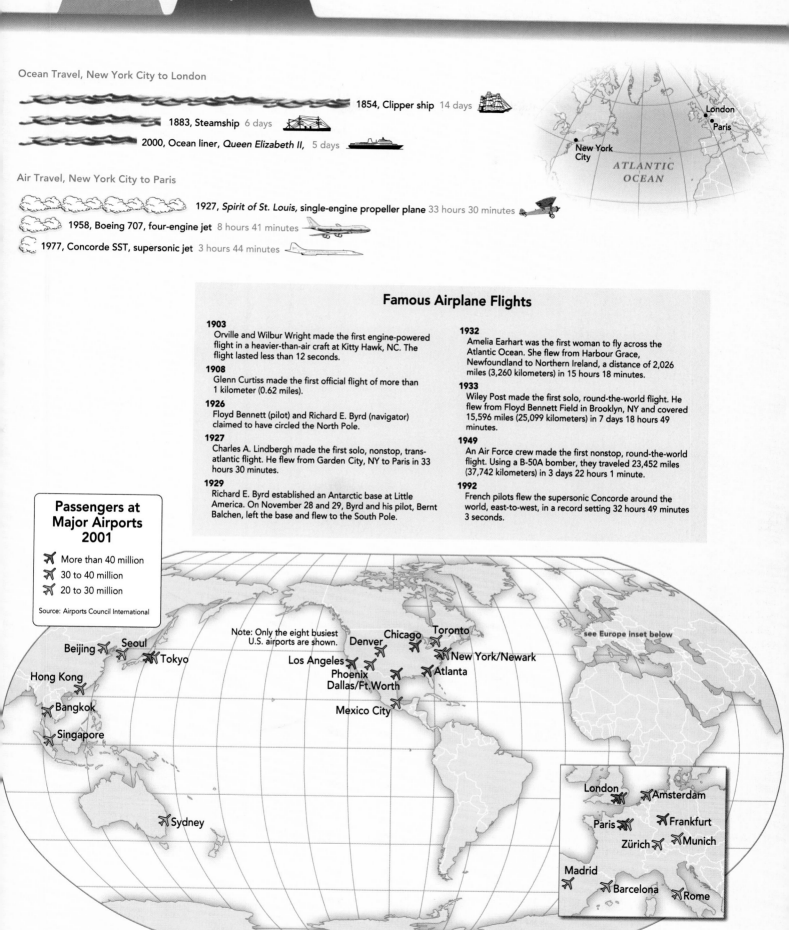

Ocean Travel, New York City to London

1854, Clipper ship 14 days

1883, Steamship 6 days

2000, Ocean liner, *Queen Elizabeth II*, 5 days

Air Travel, New York City to Paris

1927, *Spirit of St. Louis*, single-engine propeller plane 33 hours 30 minutes

1958, Boeing 707, four-engine jet 8 hours 41 minutes

1977, Concorde SST, supersonic jet 3 hours 44 minutes

London
Paris
New York City
ATLANTIC OCEAN

Famous Airplane Flights

1903
Orville and Wilbur Wright made the first engine-powered flight in a heavier-than-air craft at Kitty Hawk, NC. The flight lasted less than 12 seconds.

1908
Glenn Curtiss made the first official flight of more than 1 kilometer (0.62 miles).

1926
Floyd Bennett (pilot) and Richard E. Byrd (navigator) claimed to have circled the North Pole.

1927
Charles A. Lindbergh made the first solo, nonstop, trans-atlantic flight. He flew from Garden City, NY to Paris in 33 hours 30 minutes.

1929
Richard E. Byrd established an Antarctic base at Little America. On November 28 and 29, Byrd and his pilot, Bernt Balchen, left the base and flew to the South Pole.

1932
Amelia Earhart was the first woman to fly across the Atlantic Ocean. She flew from Harbour Grace, Newfoundland to Northern Ireland, a distance of 2,026 miles (3,260 kilometers) in 15 hours 18 minutes.

1933
Wiley Post made the first solo, round-the-world flight. He flew from Floyd Bennett Field in Brooklyn, NY and covered 15,596 miles (25,099 kilometers) in 7 days 18 hours 49 minutes.

1949
An Air Force crew made the first nonstop, round-the-world flight. Using a B-50A bomber, they traveled 23,452 miles (37,742 kilometers) in 3 days 22 hours 1 minute.

1992
French pilots flew the supersonic Concorde around the world, east-to-west, in a record setting 32 hours 49 minutes 3 seconds.

Passengers at Major Airports 2001

More than 40 million
30 to 40 million
20 to 30 million

Source: Airports Council International

Note: Only the eight busiest U.S. airports are shown.

see Europe inset below

Beijing Seoul Tokyo
Hong Kong
Bangkok
Singapore

Denver Chicago Toronto
Los Angeles New York/Newark
Phoenix Atlanta
Dallas/Ft.Worth
Mexico City

Sydney

London Amsterdam
Paris Frankfurt
Zürich Munich
Madrid
Barcelona Rome

North America

Legend:
- International boundary
- State or provincial boundary
- ⊛ National capital

Symbol and label sizes indicate relative sizes of cities:
- ● **New York**
- • Baltimore
- · Charlotte

Facts

- Area: 9,361,791 square miles (24,247,038 square kilometers)
- Highest Point: Mt. McKinley, United States, 20,320 ft. (6,194 m)
- Lowest Point: Death Valley, United States, 282 ft. (86 m) below sea level
- Longest River: Mississippi-Missouri-Red Rock, 3,710 mi. (5,971 km)
- Largest Lake: Lake Superior, United States/Canada, 31,700 sq. mi. (82,103 sq. km)
- Largest Country: Canada, 3,851,809 sq. mi. (9,976,140 sq. km)
- Largest City: New York City, United States, 21,200,000 (metropolitan population)

Nations of the Lesser Antilles

Country	Capital	Country	Capital
Antigua and Barbuda	St. John's	St. Vincent and the Grenadines	Kingstown
St. Kitts and Nevis	Basseterre	Grenada	St. George's
Dominica	Roseau	Trinidad and Tobago	Port-of-Spain
St. Lucia	Castries		
Barbados	Bridgetown		

ASIA

ARCTIC OCEAN

North + Pole

Cape Morris Jesup

EUROPE

Robinson Projection

Chukchi Sea

Bering Strait

Bering Sea

Point Barrow

Beaufort Sea

Ellesmere Island

Greenland

Denmark Strait

BROOKS RANGE

Mt. McKinley
20,320 ft.
(6,194 m)

Yukon River

ALASKA RANGE

Gulf of Alaska

Mt. Logan
19,551 ft.
(5,959 m)

MACKENZIE MTS.

Mackenzie River

Banks Island

Victoria Island

Queen Elizabeth Islands

Devon I.

Baffin Bay

Baffin Island

ARCTIC CIRCLE

Cape Farewell

Labrador Sea

Alexander Archipelago

COAST MOUNTAINS

Great Bear Lake

Great Slave Lake

Southampton I.

Davis Strait

Queen Charlotte Is.

ROCKY

Peace River

Lake Athabasca

Hudson Bay

Belcher Is.

Ungava Peninsula

Labrador

PACIFIC OCEAN

Vancouver

Fraser River

Athabasca River

Nelson R.

Anticosti I.

Newfoundland

Mt. Rainier
14,410 ft.
(4,391 m)

CASCADE RANGE

MOUNTAINS

Columbia River

Saskatchewan River

Lake Winnipeg

CANADIAN SHIELD

Gulf of St. Lawrence

Miquelon Is.

Cape Breton I.

Cape Mendocino

COAST RANGES

SIERRA NEVADA

GREAT BASIN

Snake River

GREAT PLAINS

Black Hills

Lake Superior

Lake Huron

Lake Michigan

Lake Ontario

St. Lawrence River

Niagara Falls

Lake Erie

Cape Sable

Cape Cod

ATLANTIC OCEAN

Mt. Whitney
14,494 ft.
(4,418 m)

Great Salt Lake

Death Valley
282 ft. (86 m)
below sea level

Colorado River

L. Mead

COLORADO PLATEAU

Mt. Elbert
14,433 ft.
(4,399 m)

Platte River

Missouri River

Red River

OZARK PLATEAU

Mississippi

Ohio River

Mt. Mitchell
6,684 ft.
(2,037 m)

Tennessee River

APPALACHIAN MTS.

ATLANTIC COASTAL PLAIN

Cape Hatteras

Bermuda

Arkansas

TROPIC OF CANCER

Baja California

False Cape

Gulf of California

SIERRA MADRE OCCIDENTAL

SIERRA MADRE ORIENTAL

Rio Grande

Colorado River

Brazos River

Alabama R.

GULF COASTAL PLAIN

Gulf of Mexico

Bahamas

Straits of Florida

Cuba

Cayman Is.

Jamaica

Greater Antilles

Hispaniola

Puerto Rico

Leeward Is.

Lesser Antilles

Windward Is.

Pico de Orizaba
18,405 ft.
(5,610 m)

Bay of Campeche

Yucatán Peninsula

Caribbean Sea

Aruba

Bonaire

Curaçao

Trinidad

Lake Nicaragua

Panama Canal

Isthmus of Panama

SOUTH AMERICA

0   400   800 mi
0   400   800 km

International boundary
▲ Mountain peak
▽ Lowest point
= Falls

Elevation Profile

| 12,500 ft. | Baja California | Rocky Mountains | Great Plains | Lake Michigan | Lake Huron | St. Lawrence River | Newfoundland |

7,500 ft.

2,500 ft.

Sea level

A   B

Major Metropolitan Areas

Antigua & Barbuda
St. John's — 22,000

Bahamas
Nassau — 211,000

Barbados
Bridgetown — 6,000

Belize
Belize City — 49,000
Belmopan — 8,000

Canada
Toronto — 5,030,000
Montréal — 3,549,000
Vancouver — 2,123,000
Ottawa — 1,129,000
Calgary — 993,000
Edmonton — 967,000
Québec — 698,000
Hamilton — 687,000
Winnipeg — 686,000

Costa Rica
San José — 1,305,000

Cuba
Havana — 2,192,000

Dominica
Roseau — 16,000

Dominican Republic
Santo Domingo — 2,677,000

El Salvador
San Salvador — 1,909,000

Grenada
St. George's — 5,000

Guatemala
Guatemala City — 1,007,000

Haiti
Port-au-Prince — 991,000

Honduras
Tegucigalpa — 835,000

Jamaica
Kingston — 578,000

Mexico
Mexico City — 16,203,000
Guadalajara — 3,349,000
Monterrey — 3,131,000
Puebla — 1,272,000
Ciudad Juárez — 1,187,000
Tijuana — 1,149,000
León — 1,021,000

Nicaragua
Managua — 1,148,000

Panama
Panama City — 1,002,000

Puerto Rico
San Juan — 2,450,000

St. Kitts & Nevis
Basseterre — 13,000

St. Lucia
Castries — 11,000

St. Vincent & Grenadines
Kingstown — 15,000

Trinidad & Tobago
Port of Spain — 48,000

United States
New York-Newark — 21,200,000
Los Angeles — 16,374,000
Chicago — 9,158,000
Washington-Baltimore — 7,608,000
San Francisco-Oakland-San Jose — 7,039,000
Philadelphia — 6,188,000
Boston — 5,819,000
Detroit — 5,456,000
Dallas-Ft. Worth — 5,222,000
Houston — 4,670,000
Atlanta — 4,112,000
Miami — 3,876,000
Seattle-Tacoma — 3,555,000
Phoenix — 3,252,000
Minneapolis-St. Paul — 2,969,000
Cleveland-Akron — 2,946,000
San Diego — 2,814,000
St. Louis — 2,604,000
Denver — 2,582,000
Tampa-St. Petersburg — 2,396,000
Pittsburgh — 2,359,000
Portland — 2,265,000
Cincinnati — 1,979,000
Sacramento — 1,797,000
Kansas City — 1,776,000
Milwaukee — 1,690,000

International comparability of population data is limited by varying census methods. Where metropolitan population is unavailable, core city population is shown.

Population

Persons per sq. mile	Persons per sq. km
Over 520	Over 200
260 to 519	100 to 199
130 to 259	50 to 99
25 to 129	10 to 49
1 to 24	1 to 9
0	0

Major metropolitan areas
- Over 2 million
- 1 million to 2 million
- Under 1 million

Estimated 2002 Population (in millions)

United States 281
Mexico 103
Canada 32
Guatemala 13
Cuba 11
All other countries 51

Source: U.S. Census Bureau

Electricity Use

Canada 15,748

United States 12,407

Virgin Islands 7,762

Jamaica 2,278
Mexico 1,676

El Salvador 583

KWh (kilowatt hours) per person per year

Source: *World Factbook*, CIA, 2001

Gross Domestic Product is a measure of the total goods and services generated by a country. Generally, manufacturing, high-tech services, and specialized agricultural products add more value than raw materials and basic food stuffs.

Mexico profits from oil production and a major manufacturing zone adjacent to the U.S. border, while Costa Rica has become a significant tourist destination. Haiti is the poorest country in the Western Hemisphere.

Gross Domestic Product

GDP per capita

- Over $20,000
- $10,000 to $20,000
- $5,000 to $9,999
- $2,500 to $4,999
- Under $2,500
- No data

Source: *World Factbook*, CIA, 2001

Land Use and Resources

Predominant land use

- Commercial agriculture
- Dairying
- Livestock ranching
- Subsistence agriculture
- Primarily forestland
- Limited agricultural activity

Major resources

- Coal
- Natural gas
- Oil
- Forest products
- Au Gold
- Ag Silver
- Fe Iron ore
- U Uranium
- Al Bauxite
- Other minerals
- Fishing
- Major manufacturing and trade centers

There is a profound north-south difference in North America. Canada and the U.S. are models of high-tech, globally connected economies—largely urban and service oriented societies where a relative handful of farmers produces a surplus of foodstuffs and every land use, from the irrigated fields of the West to the dairy belt of the Northeast to the forests of the North, seems to be molded by market efficiency. Without a doubt, this economic prowess has been encouraged by immense supplies of coal, oil, natural gas, wood, gold, iron ore, and other mineral resources.

Although Mexico has substantial oil and mineral resources and agricultural production that successfully struggles against challenging environmental limitations, much of its growing prosperity is linked to increased trade with the U.S., reflected in a major manufacturing zone along its northern borderlands. Central America and the Caribbean continue to wrestle with the legacy of commercial plantation agriculture and subsistence agriculture, but tourism, especially in the Caribbean, and small-scale assembly and manufacturing have become economic backbones, as well.

47

Climate

- Tropical wet
- Tropical wet and dry
- Arid
- Semiarid
- Mediterranean
- Humid subtropical
- Marine
- Humid continental
- Subarctic
- Tundra
- Highland
- Ice cap

Surrounded and enveloped by warm water, the countries of southern North America are warm and wet. The Eastern U.S. and most of Canada are striped by climate zones offering adequate precipitation and progressively lower temperatures as one travels north, but the pattern goes topsy-turvy in the West, where swirling arid and semiarid zones abut coastal regions influenced by both rain-bearing winds and cool ocean currents.

See photographs taken in different kinds of climates on pages 24–25.

Snag
Lowest recorded temperature: -81°F (-63°C)

Death Valley
Highest recorded temperature: 134°F (57°C)

Henderson Lake
Highest average annual precipitation: 256" (650 cm)

Batagues
Lowest average annual precipitation: 1.2" (3.0 cm)

Annual Precipitation

Centimeters	Inches
Over 203	Over 80
152 to 203	60 to 80
102 to 152	40 to 60
51 to 102	20 to 40
25 to 51	10 to 20
Under 25	Under 10

Just as moisture-rich trade winds sweep through the Caribbean to strike and soak Central America, prevailing westerly winds emerge from the North Pacific to collide with the coastal mountains of Canada and the U.S. Leached of rain and snow, the moving air remains dry until it once again approaches warm water—the Gulf of Mexico and the Gulf Stream enriched Atlantic Ocean.

Climate Graphs

Average daily temperature range (in °F)   Average monthly precipitation (in inches)

High / Low

ATLANTA, USA
FAIRBANKS, USA — Temp. Range -21 to -1
MEXICO CITY, Mexico
MINNEAPOLIS, USA
NUUK, Greenland
NEW YORK CITY, USA
PHOENIX, USA
ST. JOHN'S, Canada
SAN FRANCISCO, USA
SAN JOSÉ, Costa Rica
SAN JUAN, Puerto Rico
VANCOUVER, Canada

Vegetation

- Unclassified highlands or ice cap
- Tundra and alpine tundra
- Coniferous forest
- Midlatitude deciduous forest
- Subtropical broadleaf evergreen forest
- Mixed forest
- Midlatitude scrubland
- Midlatitude grassland
- Desert
- Tropical seasonal and scrub
- Tropical rain forest

Deserts spanning the U.S./Mexico border join the tropical plant life of Central America and southern Mexico to the temperate and arctic vegetation of Canada and the U.S.—vegetation predominately forest land but split by the arc of the Great Plains and interwoven with scrublands able to endure infrequent rainfall.

See photographs of different the kinds of vegetation on page 26-27.

In the U.S. and Canada, heavy consumption of energy and other resources is a source of many environmental problems. Environmental laws and regulations have helped, but air pollutants and gases continue to cause health problems and may contribute to global warming.

In the western U.S. and parts of Mexico, large areas are susceptible to desertification from overgrazing and agriculture.

Deforestation is a major issue in Latin America and the Caribbean. In Haiti, for example, all the native rain forests have been destroyed, causing irreversible harm to ecosystems.

Environmental Issues

- Current forest
- Cleared forest
- Area at highest risk of desertification
- Areas most affected by acid rain
- Poor air quality*

*Cities exceeding at least one of the World Health Organization's (WHO) annual mean guidelines for air quality

Sources: *Global Distribution of Original and Remaining Forests*, UNEP-WCMC, 2002
World Soil Resources Map Index, USDA/NRCS, 2002
World Development Indicators, World Bank, 1999

United States

Alabama

Alaska

Arizona

Arkansas

California

Hawaii

Idaho

Iowa

Kansas

Maine

Maryland

Minnesota

Mississippi

Nebraska

Nevada

New Mexico

New York

Ohio

Oklahoma

Rhode Island

South Carolina

South Dakota

Tennessee

Texas

Utah

United States

Colorado

Connecticut

Delaware

District of Columbia

Florida

Georgia

Illinois

Indiana

Kentucky

Louisiana

Massachusetts

Michigan

Missouri

Montana

New Hampshire

New Jersey

North Carolina

North Dakota

Oregon

Pennsylvania

Vermont

Virginia

Washington

West Virginia

Wisconsin

Wyoming

Facts

- Total Area: 3,717,796 square miles (9,629,091 square kilometers)
- Highest Point: Mt. McKinley, Alaska, 20,320 ft. (6,194 m)
- Lowest Point: Death Valley, California, 282 ft. (86 m) below sea level
- Longest River: Mississippi-Missouri-Red Rock, 3,710 mi. (5,971 km)
- Largest Lake (within U.S.): Lake Michigan, 22,342 sq. mi. (57,866 sq. km)
- Largest State: Alaska, 570,374 sq. mi. (1,477,268 sq. km)
- Largest City: New York City, New York, 8,008,028

Legend

- State boundary
- ✪ National capital
- ★ State capital

Symbol and label sizes indicate relative sizes of cities:
- **New York City**
- St. Louis
- Carson City

0 150 300 mi
0 150 300 km

State	2000 Population and Rank		Capital	Largest City	Abbreviation		Nickname
					Traditional	Postal Service	
Alabama	4,447,100	23rd	Montgomery	Birmingham	ALA.	AL	Heart of Dixie
Alaska	626,932	48th	Juneau	Anchorage	(none)	AK	The Last Frontier
Arizona	5,130,632	20th	Phoenix	Phoenix	ARIZ.	AZ	Grand Canyon State
Arkansas	2,673,400	33rd	Litttle Rock	Little Rock	ARK.	AR	Land of Opportunity
California	33,871,648	1st	Sacramento	Los Angeles	CALIF.	CA	Golden State
Colorado	4,301,261	24th	Denver	Denver	COLO.	CO	Centennial State
Connecticut	3,405,565	29th	Hartford	Bridgeport	CONN.	CT	Constitution State, Nutmeg State
Delaware	783,600	45th	Dover	Wilmington	DEL.	DE	First State, Diamond State
Florida	15,982,378	4th	Tallahassee	Jacksonville	FLA.	FL	Sunshine State
Georgia	8,186,453	10th	Atlanta	Atlanta	GA.	GA	Empire State of the South, Peach State
Hawaii	1,211,537	42nd	Honolulu	Honolulu	(none)	HI	Aloha State
Idaho	1,293,953	39th	Boise	Boise	IDA.	ID	Gem State
Illinois	12,419,293	5th	Springfield	Chicago	ILL.	IL	Prairie State
Indiana	6,080,485	14th	Indianapolis	Indianapolis	IND.	IN	Hoosier State
Iowa	2,926,324	30th	Des Moines	Des Moines	(none)	IA	Hawkeye State
Kansas	2,688,418	32nd	Topeka	Wichita	KANS.	KS	Sunflower State
Kentucky	4,041,769	25th	Frankfort	Louisville	KY. or KEN.	KY	Bluegrass State
Louisiana	4,468,976	22nd	Baton Rouge	New Orleans	LA.	LA	Pelican State
Maine	1,274,923	40th	Augusta	Portland	(none)	ME	Pine Tree State
Maryland	5,296,486	19th	Annapolis	Baltimore	MD.	MD	Old Line State, Free State
Massachusetts	6,349,097	13th	Boston	Boston	MASS.	MA	Bay State, Old Colony
Michigan	9,938,444	8th	Lansing	Detroit	MICH.	MI	Wolverine State
Minnesota	4,919,479	21st	St. Paul	Minneapolis	MINN.	MN	North Star State, Gopher State
Mississippi	2,844,658	31st	Jackson	Jackson	MISS.	MS	Magnolia State
Missouri	5,595,211	17th	Jefferson City	Kansas City	MO.	MO	Show Me State

State	2000 Population and Rank		Capital	Largest City	Abbreviation		Nickname
					Traditional	Postal Service	
Montana	902,195	44th	Helena	Billings	MONT.	MT	Treasure State
Nebraska	1,711,265	38th	Lincoln	Omaha	NEBR.	NE	Cornhusker State
Nevada	1,998,257	35th	Carson City	Las Vegas	NEV.	NV	Silver State
New Hampshire	1,235,786	41st	Concord	Manchester	N.H.	NH	Granite State
New Jersey	8,414,350	9th	Trenton	Newark	N.J.	NJ	Garden State
New Mexico	1,819,046	36th	Santa Fe	Albuquerque	N. MEX. or N.M.	NM	Land of Enchantment
New York	18,976,457	3rd	Albany	New York	N.Y.	NY	Empire State
North Carolina	8,049,313	11th	Raleigh	Charlotte	N.C.	NC	Tar Heel State
North Dakota	642,200	47th	Bismarck	Fargo	N. DAK. or N.D.	ND	Peace Garden State, Flickertail State
Ohio	11,353,140	7th	Columbus	Columbus	(none)	OH	Buckeye State
Oklahoma	3,450,654	27th	Oklahoma City	Oklahoma City	OKLA.	OK	Sooner State
Oregon	3,421,399	28th	Salem	Portland	ORE.	OR	Beaver State
Pennsylvania	12,281,054	6th	Harrisburg	Philadelphia	PA. or PENN.	PA	Keystone State
Rhode Island	1,048,319	43rd	Providence	Providence	R.I.	RI	Ocean State
South Carolina	4,012,012	26th	Columbia	Columbia	S.C.	SC	Palmetto State
South Dakota	754,844	46th	Pierre	Sioux Falls	S. DAK. or S.D.	SD	Mt. Rushmore State
Tennessee	5,689,283	16th	Nashville	Memphis	TENN.	TN	Volunteer State
Texas	20,851,820	2nd	Austin	Houston	TEX.	TX	Lone Star State
Utah	2,233,169	34th	Salt Lake City	Salt Lake City	(none)	UT	Beehive State
Vermont	608,827	49th	Montpelier	Burlington	VT.	VT	Green Mountain State
Virginia	7,078,515	12th	Richmond	Virginia Beach	VA.	VA	Old Dominion
Washington	5,894,121	15th	Olympia	Seattle	WASH.	WA	Evergreen State
West Virginia	1,808,344	37th	Charleston	Charleston	W. VA.	WV	Mountain State
Wisconsin	5,363,675	18th	Madison	Milwaukee	WIS.	WI	Badger State
Wyoming	493,782	50th	Cheyenne	Cheyenne	WYO.	WY	Equality State

Strait of Juan de Fuca
Cape Flattery

Legend
- International boundary
- State boundary
- ▲ Mountain peak
- ▽ Lowest point

COAST RANGES

CASCADE RANGE
Puget Sound
Columbia River
Mt. Rainier 14,410 ft. (4,391 m)
Mt. St. Helens 8,366 ft. (2,550 m)
Columbia River
Mt. Hood 11,239 ft. (3,425 m)

COLUMBIA PLATEAU
Snake River
Ouyhee River
Snake River Plain
Salmon River

BITTERROOT RANGE
Clark Fork

ROCKY
Milk River
Missouri River
Fort Peck Lake
Yellowstone River
Little Missouri River
Lake Sakakawea

Granite Peak 12,799 ft. (3,900 m)
Yellowstone Lake
Powder River
Bighorn River

GREAT
Lake Oahe
Black Hills
Cheyenne River
White R.
Niobrara River
Sand Hills

Cape Mendocino

Mt. Shasta 14,162 ft. (4,316 m)

SIERRA NEVADA
Sacramento River
Central Valley
COAST RANGES
San Joaquin River
Lake Tahoe

GREAT BASIN

Great Salt Lake
Great Salt Lake Desert

WASATCH RANGE
Green River
MOUNTAINS

Kings Peak 13,528 ft. (4,123 m)

N. Platte River
S. Platte River

FRONT RANGE

PACIFIC OCEAN

San Francisco Bay
Monterey Bay

Mt. Whitney 14,494 ft. (4,417 m)

282 ft. (86 m) below sea level
▽ Death Valley

Lake Mead

Colorado River
Lake Powell

COLORADO PLATEAU

Mt. Elbert 14,433 ft. (4,398 m)
Pikes Peak 14,110 ft. (4,629 m)

Arkansas River

SANGRE DE CRISTO
Wheeler Peak 13,161 ft. (4,011 m)

PLAINS

Point Conception

Channel Islands

Salton Sea

Mojave Desert

Sonoran Desert
Gila River

Grand Canyon

Humphreys Peak 12,633 ft. (3,850 m)
Verde River
Salt River

San Juan River

Rio Grande

Pecos River

LLANO ESTACADO

EDWARDS PLATEAU

Guadalupe Peak 8,749 ft. (2,666 m)

MEXICO

RUSSIA
Pt. Barrow
ARCTIC OCEAN
Bering Strait
BROOKS RANGE
ARCTIC CIRCLE
Seward Peninsula
St. Lawrence Island
Yukon River
RANGE
ALASKA RANGE
Mt. McKinley 20,320 ft. (6,194 m)
CANADA
Kenai Peninsula
Gulf of Alaska
Bering Sea
ALEUTIAN RANGE
Kodiak Island
Aleutian Is.

0 250 500 mi
0 250 500 km

PACIFIC OCEAN
Kauai
Niihau
Oahu
Molokai
Hawaiian
Lanai
Maui
Kahoolawe
Islands
Hawaii
Mauna Kea 13,796 ft. (4,205 m)

0 100 200 mi
0 100 200 km

Profile diagram (bottom):
Coast Ranges | Sierra Nevada | Great Basin | Wasatch Range | Mount Elbert | Pikes Peak
Lake Tahoe
15,000 ft.
10,000 ft.
5,000 ft.
Sea level A

State	Land Area and Rank		Highest Point		Temperature °F		Annual Precipitation	
					Highest Recorded	Lowest Recorded	Highest Recorded	Lowest Recorded
Alabama	50,750 sq mi 131,443 sq km	28th	Cheaha Mtn.	2,405 ft 777 m	112°	–27°	106.57"	22.00"
Alaska	570,374 sq mi 1,477,268 sq km	1st	Mt. McKinley	20,320 ft 6,194 m	100°	–80°	332.29"	1.61"
Arizona	113,642 sq mi 294,334 sq km	6th	Humphreys Peak	12,633 ft 3,851 m	128°	–40°	58.92"	0.07"
Arkansas	52,075 sq mi 134,875 sq km	27th	Magazine Mtn.	2,753 ft 839 m	120°	–29°	98.55"	19.11"
California	155,973 sq mi 403,970 sq km	3rd	Mt. Whitney	14,494 ft 4,418 m	134°	–45°	153.54"	0.00"
Colorado	103,730 sq mi 268,660 sq km	8th	Mt. Elbert	14,433 ft 4,399 m	118°	–61°	92.84"	1.69"
Connecticut	4,845 sq mi 12,550 sq km	48th	south slope of Mt. Frissell	2,380 ft 725 m	105°	–32°	78.53"	23.60"
Delaware	1,955 sq mi 5,063 sq km	49th	Ebright Road at DE-PA border	448 ft 137 m	110°	–17°	72.75"	21.38"
Florida	53,997 sq mi 139,852 sq km	26th	Sec. 30, T.6N, R.20W in Walton Co.	345 ft 105 m	109°	–2°	112.43"	21.16"
Georgia	57,919 sq mi 150,010 sq km	21st	Brasstown Bald	4,784 ft 1,458 m	112°	–17°	112.16"	17.14"
Hawaii	6,423 sq mi 16,637 sq km	47th	Pu'u Wekiu, Mauna Kea	13,796 ft 4,205 m	100°	12°	704.83"	0.19"
Idaho	82,751 sq mi 214,325 sq km	11th	Borah Peak	12,662 ft 3,859 m	118°	–60°	81.05"	2.09"
Illinois	55,593 sq mi 143,987 sq km	24th	Charles Mound	1,235 ft 376 m	117°	–35°	74.58"	16.59"
Indiana	35,870 sq mi 92,904 sq km	38th	Franklin Township in Wayne County	1,257 ft 383 m	116°	–35°	97.38"	18.67"
Iowa	55,875 sq mi 144,716 sq km	23rd	Sec. 29, T.100N, R.41W in Osceola Co.	1,670 ft 509 m	118°	–47°	74.50"	12.11"
Kansas	81,823 sq mi 211,922 sq km	13th	Mt. Sunflower	4,039 ft 1,231 m	121°	–40°	67.02"	4.77"
Kentucky	39,732 sq mi 102,907 sq km	36th	Black Mtn.	4,139 ft 1,262 m	114°	–34°	79.68"	14.51"
Louisiana	43,566 sq mi 112,836 sq km	33rd	Driskill Mtn.	535 ft 163 m	114°	–16°	113.74"	26.44"
Maine	30,865 sq mi 79,939 sq km	39th	Mt. Katahdin	5,267 ft 1,605 m	105°	–48°	75.64"	23.06"
Maryland	9,775 sq mi 25,316 sq km	42nd	Backbone Mtn.	3,360 ft 1,024 m	109°	–40°	72.59"	17.76"
Massachusetts	7,838 sq mi 20,300 sq km	45th	Mt. Greylock	3,487 ft 1,063 m	107°	–35°	72.19"	21.76"
Michigan	56,809 sq mi 147,135 sq km	22nd	Mt. Arvon	1,979 ft 603 m	112°	–51°	64.01"	15.64"
Minnesota	79,617 sq mi 206,207 sq km	14th	Eagle Mtn.	2,301 ft 701 m	114°	–59°	51.53"	7.81"
Mississippi	46,914 sq mi 121,506 sq km	31st	Woodall Mtn.	806 ft 246 m	115°	–19°	104.36"	25.97"
Missouri	68,898 sq mi 178,446 sq km	18th	Taum Sauk Mtn.	1,772 ft 540 m	118°	–40°	92.77"	16.14"

State	Land Area and Rank		Highest Point		Temperature °F		Annual Precipitation	
					Highest Recorded	Lowest Recorded	Highest Recorded	Lowest Recorded
Montana	145,556 sq mi 376,991 sq km	4th	Granite Peak	12,799 ft 3,901 m	117°	−70°	55.51"	2.97"
Nebraska	76,878 sq mi 199,113 sq km	15th	Johnson Township in Kimball County	5,424 ft 1,653 m	118°	−47°	64.52"	6.30"
Nevada	109,806 sq mi 284,397 sq km	7th	Boundary Peak	13,140 ft 4,005 m	125°	−50°	59.03"	Trace
New Hampshire	8,969 sq mi 23,231 sq km	44th	Mt. Washington	6,288 ft 1,917 m	106°	−46°	130.14"	22.31"
New Jersey	7,419 sq mi 19,215 sq km	46th	High Point	1,803 ft 550 m	110°	−34°	85.99"	19.85"
New Mexico	121,365 sq mi 314,334 sq km	5th	Wheeler Peak	13,161 ft 4,011 m	122°	−50°	62.45"	1.00"
New York	47,224 sq mi 122,310 sq km	30th	Mt. Marcy	5,344 ft 1,629 m	108°	−52°	82.06"	17.64"
North Carolina	48,718 sq mi 126,180 sq km	29th	Mt. Mitchell	6,684 ft 2,037 m	110°	−34°	129.60"	22.69"
North Dakota	68,994 sq mi 178,695 sq km	17th	White Butte	3,506 ft 1,069 m	121°	−60°	37.98"	4.02"
Ohio	40,953 sq mi 106,067 sq km	35th	Campbell Hill	1,549 ft 472 m	113°	−39°	70.82"	16.96"
Oklahoma	68,679 sq mi 177,878 sq km	19th	Black Mesa	4,973 ft 1,516 m	120°	−27°	84.47"	6.53"
Oregon	96,003 sq mi 248,647 sq km	10th	Mt. Hood	11,239 ft 3,426 m	119°	−54°	168.88"	3.33"
Pennsylvania	44,820 sq mi 116,083 sq km	32nd	Mt. Davis	3,213 ft 979 m	111°	−42°	81.64"	15.71"
Rhode Island	1,045 sq mi 2,707 sq km	50th	Jerimoth Hill	812 ft 247 m	104°	−23°	70.21"	24.08"
South Carolina	30,111 sq mi 77,988 sq km	40th	Sassafras Mtn.	3,560 ft 1,085 m	111°	−19°	101.65"	20.73"
South Dakota	75,891 sq mi 196,575 sq km	16th	Harney Peak	7,242 ft 2,207 m	120°	−58°	48.42"	2.89"
Tennessee	41,220 sq mi 106,759 sq km	34th	Clingmans Dome	6,643 ft 2,025 m	113°	−32°	114.88"	25.23"
Texas	261,914 sq mi 678,358 sq km	2nd	Guadalupe Peak	8,749 ft 2,667 m	120°	−23°	109.38"	1.64"
Utah	82,168 sq mi 212,816 sq km	12th	Kings Peak	13,528 ft 4,123 m	117°	−69°	108.54"	1.34"
Vermont	9,249 sq mi 23,956 sq km	43rd	Mt. Mansfield	4,393 ft 1,339 m	105°	−50°	92.88"	22.98"
Virginia	35,598 sq mi 102,558 sq km	37th	Mt. Rogers	5,729 ft 1,746 m	110°	−30°	81.78"	12.52"
Washington	66,582 sq mi 172,447 sq km	20th	Mt. Rainier	14,410 ft 4,392 m	118°	−48°	184.56"	2.61"
West Virginia	24,087 sq mi 62,384 sq km	41st	Spruce Knob	4,861 ft 1,481 m	112°	−37°	94.01"	9.50"
Wisconsin	54,314 sq mi 104,673 sq km	25th	Timms Hill	1,951 ft 595 m	114°	−54°	62.07"	12.00"
Wyoming	97,105 sq mi 251,501 sq km	9th	Gannett Peak	13,804 ft 4,207 m	114°	−63°	55.46"	1.28"

Divide

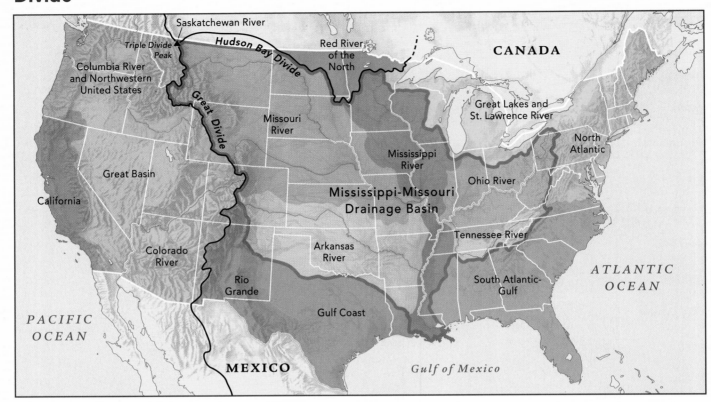

DIVIDE: *The boundary or high ground between river systems.* Streams on one side of the divide flow in a different direction and into a different drainage basin from the streams on the other side. A continental divide is the boundary that separates the rivers flowing toward opposite sides of a continent.

In North America a continental divide called the **Great Divide** runs along the crest of the Rocky Mountains, dividing rivers that flow to the Gulf of Mexico and the Atlantic Ocean from those that flow into the Pacific Ocean. Another much lower divide separates those rivers that flow north through Hudson Bay to the Arctic Ocean. Triple Divide Peak in Montana is located on both these divides. Water from one side of this mountain flows east to the Atlantic; from another side water flows west to the Pacific; and from the north face, water flows to the Arctic Ocean.

Earthquakes

- ■ Major earthquake
- • Other earthquake

The major earthquakes that have occurred in California are distributed along the major fault lines depicted on the California map to the right.

Fall Line

FALL LINE: *A geologic feature where uplands meet lowlands and a series of waterfalls and rapids occur.* Fall lines are formed where a region of hard rock borders softer rock, and the softer rock has eroded away. The erosion creates a ledge that water flows over.

A major fall line exists in the eastern United States. It marks the boundary between the Coastal Plain and the Piedmont and runs between New York and Alabama. Cities have grown into industrial and commercial hubs around each waterfall on the fall line for two reasons. First, the energy of the falling water can be captured and used by industry. Second, the fall line is often the farthest point reachable by ships carrying goods up river, which means that goods are transferred to land-based transport at that point. Some fall line cities on the East Coast include Trenton, Philadelphia, Baltimore, Washington, D.C., Richmond, Petersburg, Columbia, Macon, and Montgomery. If you draw a line on a map connecting these city dots, you will have drawn the Eastern Fall Line.

Fault

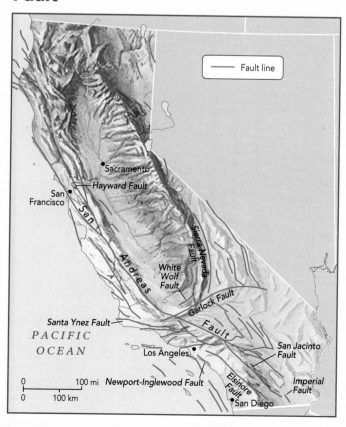

FAULT: *A break in the Earth's crust caused by movement.* Solid rock on one side of the fault no longer matches the solid rock on the other side. The movement may take place in any direction—up, down, or sideways. The movement may be a few inches or thousands of feet.

A fault that moves up or down is called a **dip-slip fault**. Niagara Falls cascades over an escarpment caused by this kind of movement.

A fault that moves sideways is called a **strike-slip fault**. The San Andreas fault is an example of this kind. Horizontal movement along this fault caused the devastating San Francisco earthquake in 1906 and will cause more earthquakes in the future. This happens because this fault marks the boundary between the Pacific Plate and the North American Plate (see page 20).

Where two parallel faults pull away from each other, they create a long, sunken valley between them called a **rift**. The Great Rift Valley in Africa is the world's most visible example (see page 91). Underwater, the huge Mid-Ocean Ridge is the longest rift on Earth (see pages 18–19).

Marine

Quillayute
Most annual
cloudy days: 240

Mt. Baker
Most snow in one season:
1,140" (2,896 cm), 1998–1999

Astoria
Most annual
cloudy days: 240

Highland

Seattle

WASHINGTON

Portland

OREGON

MONTANA

Helena

NORTH DAKOTA

IDAHO

Boise

WYOMING

SOUTH DAKOTA

Mediterranean

Reno

NEVADA

Salt Lake
City

UTAH

Silver Lake
Most snow in 24 hours:
75.8" (192.5 cm), 1921

Denver

NEBRASKA

San Francisco

COLORADO

KANSAS

CALIFORNIA

Death Valley
Highest recorded
temperature: 134°F (57°C), 1913

Death Valley
Lowest average annual
precipitation, 2.25" (5.7 cm)

Los Angeles

ARIZONA

NEW
MEXICO

Tundra

San Diego

Yuma
Daily chance of sunshine: 90%

Phoenix

OKLAHOMA

Prospect Creek Camp
Lowest recorded
temperature:
-80°F (-62°C), 1917

Fairbanks

ALASKA

Anchorage

Dallas

TEXAS

San Antonio

Arid

Mt. Waialeale
Highest average annual precipitation:
460.0" (1,168 cm)

Honolulu

HAWAII

Subarctic

Tropical wet

Hilo

Hilo
Most days
of rain: 277

Semiarid

Humid continental

Climate

- Tropical wet
- Tropical wet and dry
- Arid
- Semiarid
- Mediterranean
- Humid subtropical
- Marine
- Humid continental
- Subarctic
- Tundra
- Highland

Humid subtropical

Tropical wet and dry

Mt. Washington
Highest wind gust:
231 mph (372 kph), 1934

Blue Hill
Highest average annual wind speed:
15.4 mph (24.8 kph)

Johnstown
Deadliest flood: over 2,200 dead, 1889

Great Midwest Flood
Costliest flood damage: $18 billion, 1993

Tri-State Tornado
Deadliest tornado: 689 dead, 1925

Alvin
Most rain in 24 hours:
43.0" (109.2 cm), 1979

Galveston
Deadliest hurricane: over 8,000 dead, 1900

Hurricane Andrew
Costliest hurricane
damage: $26.5 billion,
1992

MAINE
Portland
VT
NH
Boston
MA
RI
CT
New York City
NEW JERSEY
DELAWARE
MARYLAND

MINNESOTA
Minneapolis
WISCONSIN
Lake Superior
MICHIGAN
Lake Michigan
Lake Huron
Lake Ontario
Buffalo
NEW YORK
PENNSYLVANIA
Philadelphia
Detroit
Lake Erie
Chicago
IOWA
ILLINOIS
INDIANA
OHIO
Indianapolis
MISSOURI
St. Louis
WEST VIRGINIA
Washington, D.C.
Baltimore
VIRGINIA
KENTUCKY
Lexington
Nashville
TENNESSEE
Raleigh
NORTH CAROLINA
ARKANSAS
SOUTH CAROLINA
Atlanta
MISSISSIPPI
GEORGIA
ALABAMA
LOUISIANA
New Orleans
Houston
FLORIDA
Miami

Midlatitude grassland

Coniferous forest

WASHINGTON

Seattle

Portland

OREGON

MONTANA

Helena

NORTH DAKOTA

IDAHO

Boise

SOUTH DAKOTA

WYOMING

NEVADA

Reno

Salt Lake City

NEBRASKA

San Francisco

UTAH

Denver

COLORADO

CALIFORNIA

KANSAS

Los Angeles

San Diego

ARIZONA

Phoenix

NEW MEXICO

OKLAHOMA

Dallas

TEXAS

San Antonio

Midlatitude scrubland

Tundra

Desert

ALASKA

Anchorage

Honolulu

HAWAII

Tropical rain forest

MINNESOTA

Lake Superior

MICHIGAN

Lake Huron

Minneapolis

WISCONSIN

Lake Michigan

MAINE

VERMONT
Portland

NEW
HAMPSHIRE

MASSACHUSETTS
Boston

Lake Ontario

Buffalo

NEW YORK

RHODE ISLAND
CONNECTICUT

IOWA

Detroit

Lake Erie

Chicago

OHIO

PENNSYLVANIA

New York City

NEW JERSEY

Philadelphia

ILLINOIS   INDIANA

Indianapolis

Baltimore

Washington, D.C.

DELAWARE

MARYLAND

WEST
VIRGINIA

VIRGINIA

St. Louis

MISSOURI

Lexington

KENTUCKY

Raleigh

NORTH CAROLINA

ARKANSAS

Nashville

TENNESSEE

SOUTH
CAROLINA

Atlanta

MISSISSIPPI

ALABAMA

GEORGIA

LOUISIANA

Houston

New Orleans

FLORIDA

Miami

Deciduous forest

Vegetation

- Tundra and alpine tundra
- Coniferous forest
- Midlatitude deciduous forest
- Subtropical broadleaf evergreen forest
- Mixed forest
- Midlatitude scrubland
- Midlatitude grassland
- Desert
- Tropical rain forest

Mixed forest

Subtropical broadleaf evergreen forest

Land Use

- Farming
- Grazing
- Primarily forestland
- Limited agricultural activity
- Urban area

Seattle
Tacoma
WASHINGTON
Portland
OREGON
MONTANA
IDAHO
NORTH DAKOTA
SOUTH DAKOTA
WYOMING
Salt Lake City
NEVADA
Sacramento
San Francisco
Oakland
San Jose
CALIFORNIA
UTAH
Denver
COLORADO
NEBRASKA
KANSAS
Wichita
Las Vegas
Los Angeles
San Bernardino
ARIZONA
Phoenix
Albuquerque
NEW MEXICO
OKLAHOM
Oklahoma City
San Diego
El Paso
Dalla
Fort Worth
TEXAS
San Antonio

ALASKA
Anchorage

Honolulu
HAWAII

Leading Agricultural States

CA	$25,510
TX	$13,344
IA	$10,774
NE	$8,952
KS	$7,905
MN	$7,522

Farm income in millions of dollars

Source: Economic Research Service, 2000 data, U.S. Dept. of Agriculture

Leading Corn Producing States

IL	$3,170
IA	$3,045
NE	$1,978
MN	$1,675
IN	$1,509
OH	$970

Value in millions of dollars

Leading Soy Producing States

IL	$2,230
IA	$2,181
MN	$1,348
IN	$1,230
OH	$895
MO	$831

Value in millions of dollars

Leading Wheat Producing States

KS	$939
ND	$907
WA	$459
MT	$438
OK	$386
SD	$318

Value in millions of dollars

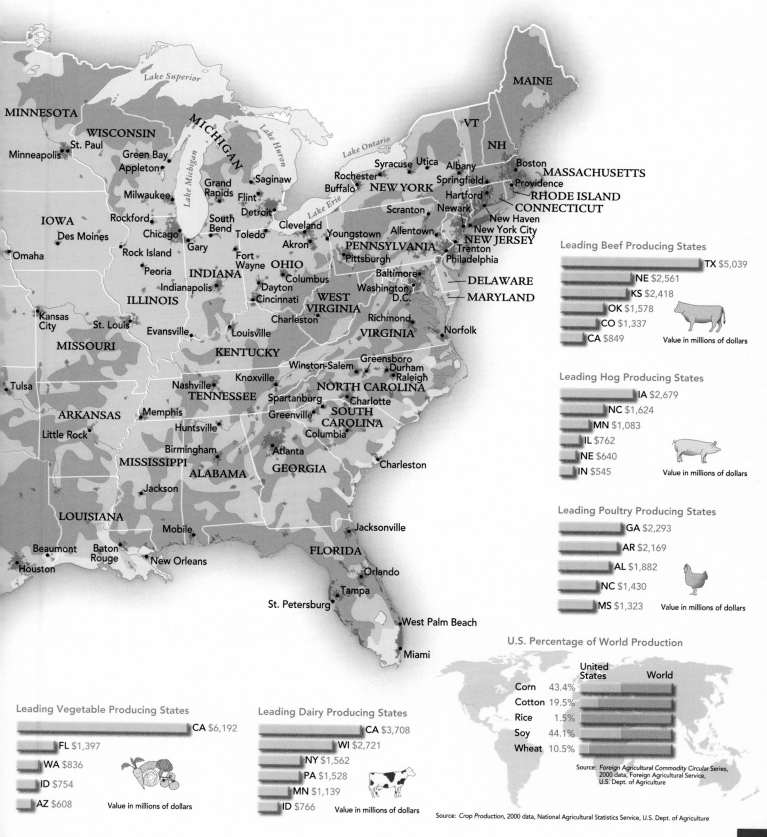

MAINE

MINNESOTA

WISCONSIN

MICHIGAN

Lake Superior

Lake Michigan

Lake Huron

Lake Ontario

Lake Erie

VT

NH

St. Paul
Minneapolis

Green Bay
Appleton

Milwaukee

Grand Rapids

Flint

Saginaw

Rockford

South Bend

IOWA

Des Moines

Omaha

Chicago

Gary

Rock Island

Peoria

INDIANA

Detroit

Toledo

Cleveland

Akron

Youngstown

OHIO

Columbus

Dayton

Cincinnati

Indianapolis

ILLINOIS

Kansas City

St. Louis

MISSOURI

Evansville

Louisville

KENTUCKY

WEST VIRGINIA

Charleston

Tulsa

Nashville

Knoxville

TENNESSEE

ARKANSAS

Memphis

Little Rock

Huntsville

Spartanburg

Greenville

Birmingham

MISSISSIPPI

ALABAMA

Jackson

Atlanta

GEORGIA

Columbia

SOUTH CAROLINA

NORTH CAROLINA

Winston-Salem

Greensboro
Durham
Raleigh

Charlotte

VIRGINIA

Richmond

Norfolk

Washington, D.C.

Baltimore

MARYLAND

DELAWARE

Philadelphia

Trenton

NEW JERSEY

NEW YORK

PENNSYLVANIA

Pittsburgh

Scranton

Allentown

Buffalo

Rochester

Syracuse

Utica

Albany

Springfield

Hartford

Newark

New Haven

New York City

CONNECTICUT

RHODE ISLAND

Providence

Boston

MASSACHUSETTS

LOUISIANA

Beaumont

Baton Rouge

New Orleans

Houston

Mobile

FLORIDA

Jacksonville

Orlando

Tampa

St. Petersburg

West Palm Beach

Miami

Leading Beef Producing States

TX $5,039
NE $2,561
KS $2,418
OK $1,578
CO $1,337
CA $849

Value in millions of dollars

Leading Hog Producing States

IA $2,679
NC $1,624
MN $1,083
IL $762
NE $640
IN $545

Value in millions of dollars

Leading Poultry Producing States

GA $2,293
AR $2,169
AL $1,882
NC $1,430
MS $1,323

Value in millions of dollars

Leading Vegetable Producing States

CA $6,192
FL $1,397
WA $836
ID $754
AZ $608

Value in millions of dollars

Leading Dairy Producing States

CA $3,708
WI $2,721
NY $1,562
PA $1,528
MN $1,139
ID $766

Value in millions of dollars

U.S. Percentage of World Production

United States | World

Corn   43.4%
Cotton 19.5%
Rice   1.5%
Soy   44.1%
Wheat   10.5%

Source: Foreign Agricultural Commodity Circular Series, 2000 data, Foreign Agricultural Service, U.S. Dept. of Agriculture

Source: Crop Production, 2000 data, National Agricultural Statistics Service, U.S. Dept. of Agriculture

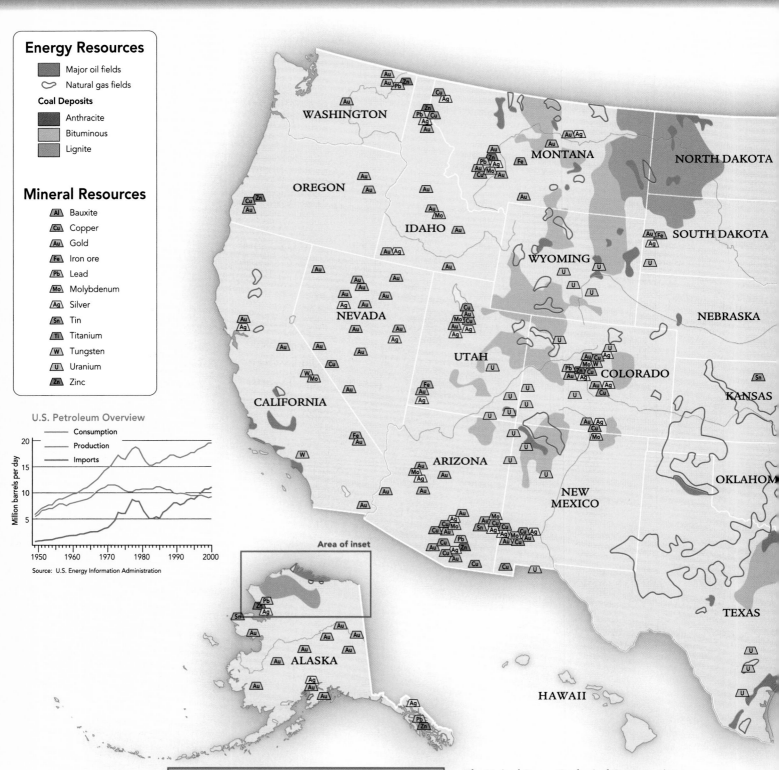

Energy Resources

- Major oil fields
- Natural gas fields

Coal Deposits
- Anthracite
- Bituminous
- Lignite

Mineral Resources

- Al Bauxite
- Cu Copper
- Au Gold
- Fe Iron ore
- Pb Lead
- Mo Molybdenum
- Ag Silver
- Sn Tin
- Ti Titanium
- W Tungsten
- U Uranium
- Zn Zinc

U.S. Petroleum Overview

- Consumption
- Production
- Imports

Source: U.S. Energy Information Administration

The United States Geological Survey estimates that there is a 50% chance of extracting 5 billion barrels of oil from the coastal plain within the Arctic National Wildlife Refuge. Debate surrounds the issue of drilling and production and its impact on the environment.

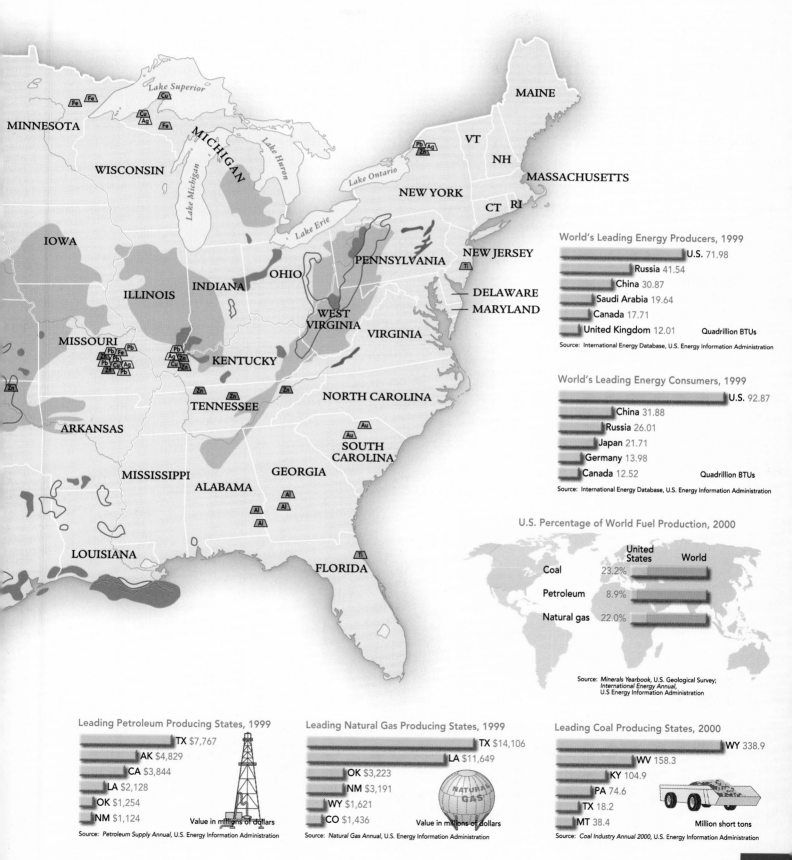

MAINE

MINNESOTA

Fe | Fe

Cu

Lake Superior

Cu
Ag

Fe

WISCONSIN

MICHIGAN

Lake Huron

Lake Michigan

VT

NH

MASSACHUSETTS

Pb | Ag
Zn

Lake Ontario

NEW YORK

CT | RI

IOWA

Lake Erie

PENNSYLVANIA

OHIO

NEW JERSEY

Ti

ILLINOIS

INDIANA

DELAWARE

MARYLAND

MISSOURI

Pb | Fe
Zn | Pb
Pb | Cu | Ag
Zn | Pb

Pb
Ag | Zn
Cu | Zn

WEST
VIRGINIA

VIRGINIA

KENTUCKY

Zn

Zn

Zn

Zn

NORTH CAROLINA

ARKANSAS

TENNESSEE

Au

Au

SOUTH
CAROLINA

MISSISSIPPI

ALABAMA

GEORGIA

Al

Al | Al

Al | Al

LOUISIANA

FLORIDA

Ti

World's Leading Energy Producers, 1999

U.S. 71.98
Russia 41.54
China 30.87
Saudi Arabia 19.64
Canada 17.71
United Kingdom 12.01   Quadrillion BTUs

Source: International Energy Database, U.S. Energy Information Administration

World's Leading Energy Consumers, 1999

U.S. 92.87
China 31.88
Russia 26.01
Japan 21.71
Germany 13.98
Canada 12.52   Quadrillion BTUs

Source: International Energy Database, U.S. Energy Information Administration

U.S. Percentage of World Fuel Production, 2000

	United States	World
Coal	23.2%	
Petroleum	8.9%	
Natural gas	22.0%	

Source: Minerals Yearbook, U.S. Geological Survey;
International Energy Annual,
U.S Energy Information Administration

Leading Petroleum Producing States, 1999

TX $7,767
AK $4,829
CA $3,844
LA $2,128
OK $1,254
NM $1,124   Value in millions of dollars

Source: Petroleum Supply Annual, U.S. Energy Information Administration

Leading Natural Gas Producing States, 1999

TX $14,106
LA $11,649
OK $3,223
NM $3,191
WY $1,621
CO $1,436   Value in millions of dollars

NATURAL GAS

Source: Natural Gas Annual, U.S. Energy Information Administration

Leading Coal Producing States, 2000

WY 338.9
WV 158.3
KY 104.9
PA 74.6
TX 18.2
MT 38.4   Million short tons

Source: Coal Industry Annual 2000, U.S. Energy Information Administration

North America

The United States

Canada

Mexico

South America

Europe

WA

Seattle
Olympia
Tacoma
Spokane

OR
Portland
Salem
Eugene

MT
Helena

ND
Bismarck

Boise

ID

WY

SD
Pierre

Reno
Carson City
NV

PACIFIC TIME ZONE
MOUNTAIN TIME ZONE

Salt Lake City

Cheyenne

NE

San Francisco
Oakland
Sacramento
Stockton
San Jose
Salinas
CA
Fresno

UT

Denver
Colorado Springs
CO

Las Vegas

KS
Wichita

Bakersfield

MOUNTAIN T.Z.
CENTRAL T.Z.

Los Angeles
Long Beach
San Bernardino
Riverside
San Diego

AZ

Phoenix

Santa Fe
Albuquerque

Amarillo

OK
Oklahoma City

NM

Lubbock

Tucson

El Paso

Abilene
Ft. Worth
Dall
TX
Waco

Austin

Barrow

ALASKA TIME ZONE

Nome
Circle
Fairbanks

ALASKA

Bethel
Anchorage
Valdez
Haines
Skagway
Homer
Seward
Juneau
Kodiak
Ketchikan

San Antonio

Laredo

Niihau
Kauai
Lihue
Oahu
Kaneohe
Honolulu
Lahaina
Molokai
Kahului
Lanai
Maui
Kahoolawe

HAWAII
HAWAII-ALEUTIAN TIME ZONE

Kailua-Kona
Hilo
Hawaii

Brownsville
Corpus Christi

0   200   400 mi
0   200   400 km

0   100 mi
0   100 km

Transportation

— Limited access (free)
— Limited access (toll)
— Primary highway
— Amtrak
— Time zone boundary
⬭90 Interstate highway
⬡51 U.S. highway
⬢86 State highway
◉ National capital
★ State capital
⊙ Other city
✈ Busiest airports (based on passenger arrivals and departures)

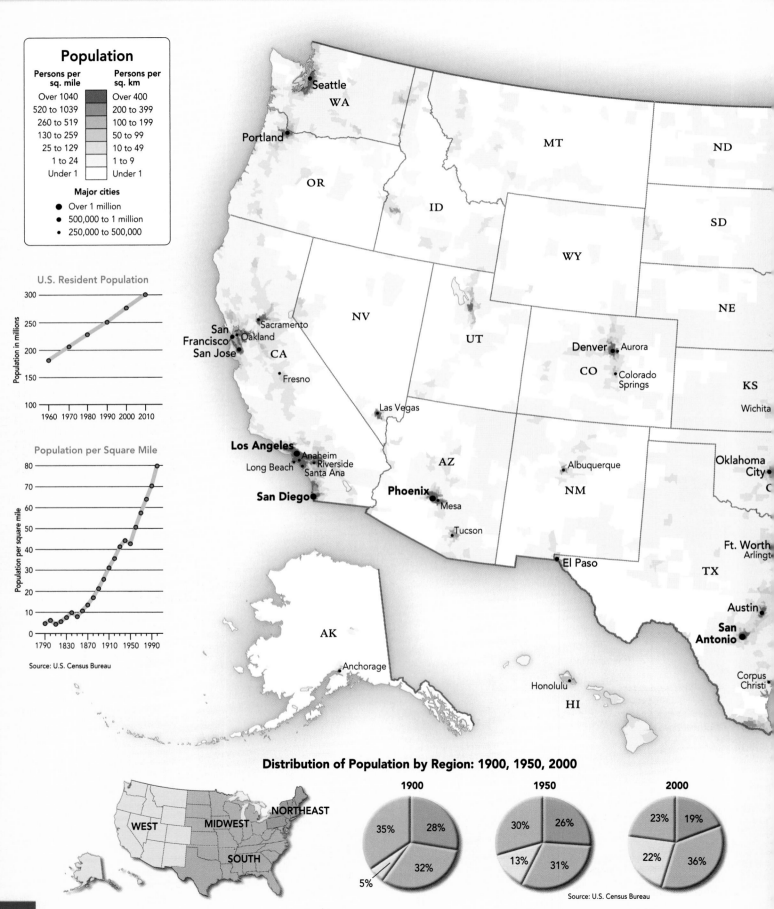

Population

Persons per sq. mile / **Persons per sq. km**

Over 1040	Over 400
520 to 1039	200 to 399
260 to 519	100 to 199
130 to 259	50 to 99
25 to 129	10 to 49
1 to 24	1 to 9
Under 1	Under 1

Major cities
- ● Over 1 million
- ● 500,000 to 1 million
- • 250,000 to 500,000

U.S. Resident Population
Population in millions: 100, 150, 200, 250, 300
Years: 1960, 1970, 1980, 1990, 2000, 2010

Population per Square Mile
Population per square mile: 0, 10, 20, 30, 40, 50, 60, 70, 80
Years: 1790, 1830, 1870, 1910, 1950, 1990

Source: U.S. Census Bureau

Distribution of Population by Region: 1900, 1950, 2000

WEST, MIDWEST, NORTHEAST, SOUTH

1900: West 5%, Midwest 35%, Northeast 28%, South 32%
1950: West 13%, Midwest 30%, Northeast 26%, South 31%
2000: West 22%, Midwest 23%, Northeast 19%, South 36%

Source: U.S. Census Bureau

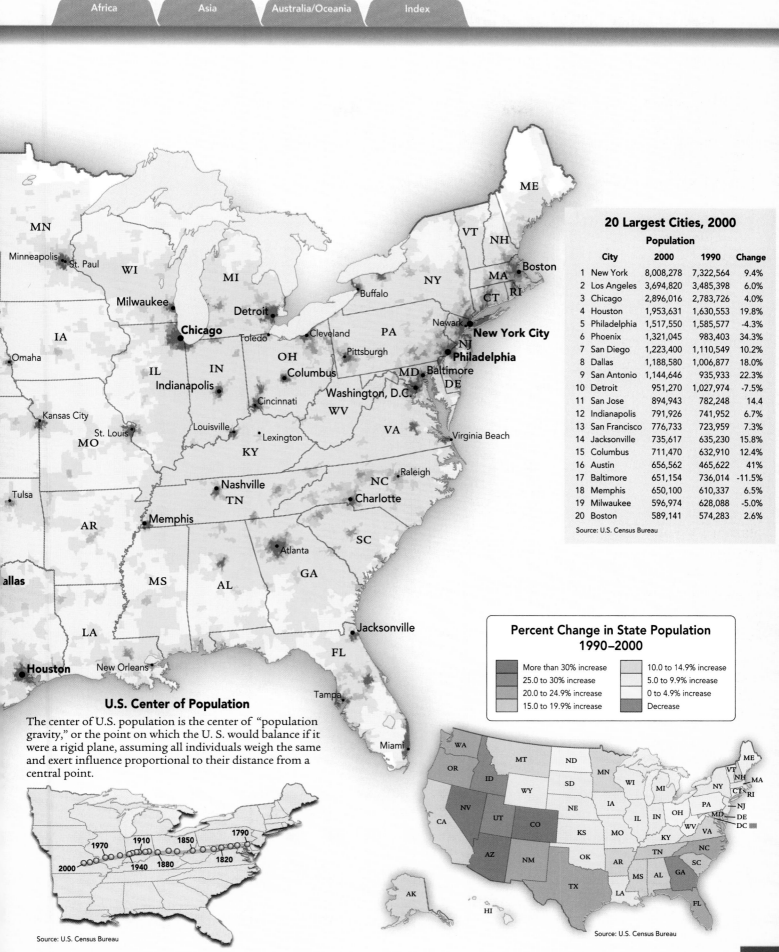

20 Largest Cities, 2000

Population

	City	2000	1990	Change
1	New York	8,008,278	7,322,564	9.4%
2	Los Angeles	3,694,820	3,485,398	6.0%
3	Chicago	2,896,016	2,783,726	4.0%
4	Houston	1,953,631	1,630,553	19.8%
5	Philadelphia	1,517,550	1,585,577	-4.3%
6	Phoenix	1,321,045	983,403	34.3%
7	San Diego	1,223,400	1,110,549	10.2%
8	Dallas	1,188,580	1,006,877	18.0%
9	San Antonio	1,144,646	935,933	22.3%
10	Detroit	951,270	1,027,974	-7.5%
11	San Jose	894,943	782,248	14.4
12	Indianapolis	791,926	741,952	6.7%
13	San Francisco	776,733	723,959	7.3%
14	Jacksonville	735,617	635,230	15.8%
15	Columbus	711,470	632,910	12.4%
16	Austin	656,562	465,622	41%
17	Baltimore	651,154	736,014	-11.5%
18	Memphis	650,100	610,337	6.5%
19	Milwaukee	596,974	628,088	-5.0%
20	Boston	589,141	574,283	2.6%

Source: U.S. Census Bureau

U.S. Center of Population

The center of U.S. population is the center of "population gravity," or the point on which the U. S. would balance if it were a rigid plane, assuming all individuals weigh the same and exert influence proportional to their distance from a central point.

Source: U.S. Census Bureau

Percent Change in State Population 1990–2000

- More than 30% increase
- 25.0 to 30% increase
- 20.0 to 24.9% increase
- 15.0 to 19.9% increase
- 10.0 to 14.9% increase
- 5.0 to 9.9% increase
- 0 to 4.9% increase
- Decrease

Source: U.S. Census Bureau

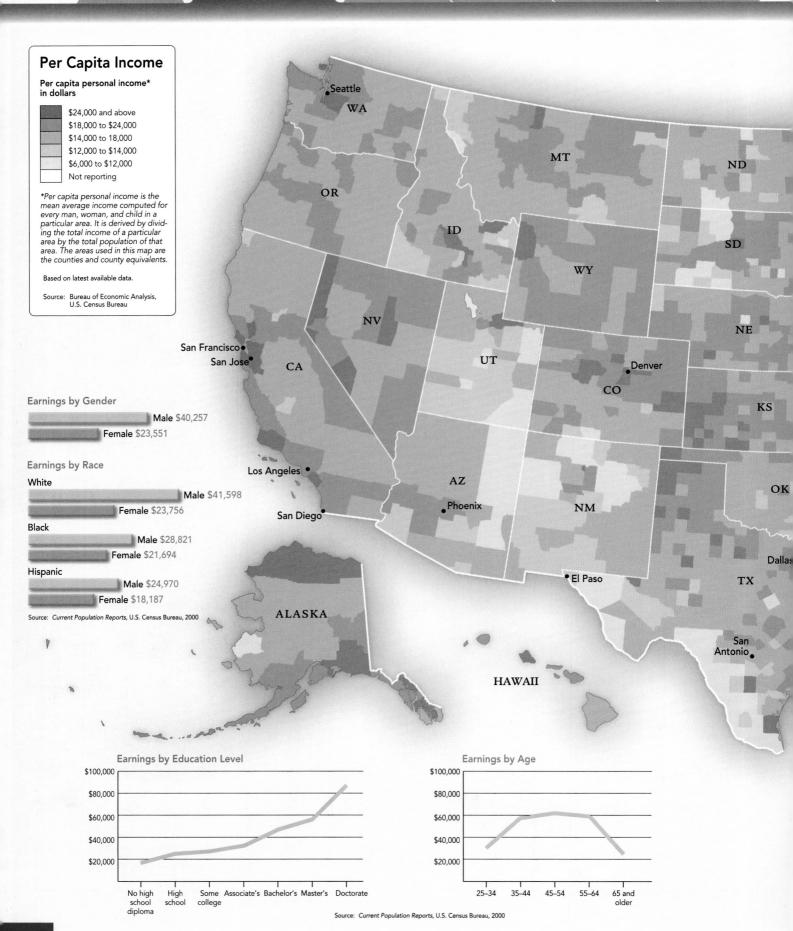

Per Capita Income

Per capita personal income*
in dollars

- $24,000 and above
- $18,000 to $24,000
- $14,000 to 18,000
- $12,000 to $14,000
- $6,000 to $12,000
- Not reporting

*Per capita personal income is the mean average income computed for every man, woman, and child in a particular area. It is derived by dividing the total income of a particular area by the total population of that area. The areas used in this map are the counties and county equivalents.

Based on latest available data.

Source: Bureau of Economic Analysis, U.S. Census Bureau

Earnings by Gender

Male $40,257
Female $23,551

Earnings by Race

White
Male $41,598
Female $23,756

Black
Male $28,821
Female $21,694

Hispanic
Male $24,970
Female $18,187

Source: *Current Population Reports,* U.S. Census Bureau, 2000

Earnings by Education Level

$100,000
$80,000
$60,000
$40,000
$20,000

No high school diploma | High school | Some college | Associate's | Bachelor's | Master's | Doctorate

Earnings by Age

$100,000
$80,000
$60,000
$40,000
$20,000

25–34 | 35–44 | 45–54 | 55–64 | 65 and older

Source: *Current Population Reports,* U.S. Census Bureau, 2000

MN

WI

MI

IA

IL

IN

MO

KY

AR

TN

MS

AL

LA

Houston

Milwaukee

Chicago

Detroit

Cleveland

Columbus

Indianapolis

Memphis

OH

WV

VA

NC

SC

GA

FL

Jacksonville

PA

NY

ME

VT

NH

MA · Boston

CT RI

NJ

New York City

Philadelphia

MD Baltimore

DE

Washington, D.C.

Highest Per Capita Income*

Luxembourg $36,400
United States $36,200
Bermuda $33,000
San Marino $32,000
Switzerland $28,600
Aruba $28,000
Norway $27,700
Monaco $27,000
Singapore $26,500
Denmark $25,500
Belgium $25,300
Austria $25,000
Japan $24,900
Canada $24,800
Iceland $24,800
France $24,400
Netherlands $24,400
Germany $23,400
Australia $23,200

*estimated, 2000

Source: *The World Factbook 2000,* CIA

Persons Below the Poverty Level

- 30% and above
- 25% to 30%
- 20% to 25%
- 15% to 20%
- 10% to 15%
- Less than 10%

Poverty level is based on the income a household needs so that no more than a third of income must be used for adequate food. Households with incomes below this level are considered to be poor. The U.S. government adjusts the poverty level according to household size, and revises it each year for changes in the cost of living.

Source: Census 2000, U.S. Census Bureau

Canada

Facts

- Area: 3,511,022 square miles (9,093,507 square kilometers)
- Highest Point: Mt. Logan, 19,551 ft. (5,959 m)
- Lowest Point: sea level
- Longest River: Mackenzie, 1,023 mi. (1,730 km)
- Largest Lake: Great Bear Lake, 12,096 sq. mi. (31,328 sq. km)
- Largest City: Toronto, Ontario, 2,481,494 (city population)

Legend

International boundary
Provincial boundary
⊛ National capital
★ Other capital

Symbol and label sizes indicate relative sizes of cities:

Toronto
Vancouver
Sault Ste. Marie

All offshore islands in Hudson Bay, James Bay, Ungava Bay, and Hudson Strait are part of Nunavut

Québec

Nunavut

Newfoundland and Labrador

Prince Edward Island

Nova Scotia

New Brunswick

Ontario

Manitoba

Saskatchewan

Alberta

British Columbia

Northwest Territories

Yukon Territory

Canada

Mexico

Facts

- Area: 742,490 square miles (1,923,040 square kilometers)
- Highest Point: Pico de Orizaba, 18,405 ft. (5,610 m)
- Lowest Point: Laguna Salada, 33 ft. (10 m) below sea level
- Longest River: Rio Bravo del Norte, 1,240 mi. (1,996 km), along U.S. border
- Largest Lake: Lake Chapala, 417 sq. mi. (1,080 sq. km)
- Largest City: Mexico City, Distrito Federal, 8,489,007

Mexico (flag)

México · Jalisco · Campeche · Coahuila · Distrito Federal · Guanajuato · Hidalgo · Nayarit · Sinaloa · Zacatecas · Yucatán · Veracruz · Tlaxcala · San Luis Potosí · Tamaulipas · Baja California Sur · Chihuahua · Colima · Baja California · Chiapas · Querétaro · Tabasco · Sonora · Aguascalientes · Puebla · Quintana Roo · Morelos · Oaxaca · Durango · Guerrero · Michoacán · Nuevo León

Legend:
- International boundary
- State boundary
- ⊛ National capital
- ★ Other capital

Symbol and label sizes indicate relative sizes of cities:
- **Mexico City**
- • Veracruz
- Cancún

PACIFIC
OCEAN

PACIFIC
OCEAN

EUROPE
ASIA
AUSTRALIA

ATLANTIC
OCEAN

ARCTIC OCEAN

NORTH
AMERICA

AFRICA

INDIAN
OCEAN

ANTARCTICA

SOUTH
AMERICA

PACIFIC
OCEAN

Equator

Robinson Projection

International boundary
Mountain peak
Lowest point

CUBA

Yucatán Channel

Cozumel I.
Point Allen
Point Herrero

Cape
Catoche

Chetumal
Bay

BELIZE

TROPIC OF CANCER

Yucatán
Peninsula

GUATEMALA

Términos
Lagoon

Usumacinta R.

Angostura
Reservoir

SIERRA MADRE
DE CHIAPAS

Point
Zapotitlán

Grijalva R.

Nezahualcóyotl
Reservoir

Isthmus of
Tehuantepec

Gulf of
Tehuantepec

Gulf of Mexico

Bay of
Campeche

Madre Lagoon

Cape Rojo

Tamiahua
Lagoon

Pánuco R.

SIERRA
AZUL

Pico de Orizaba
18,405 ft.
(5,610 m)

Miguel Alemán
Reservoir

OAXACA
PLATEAU

Verde R.

Atoyac R.

Ixtachuatl
17,343 ft.
(5,286 m)

Popocatépetl
17,887 ft.
(5,452 m)

UNITED STATES

SIERRA MADRE ORIENTAL

Falcon
Reservoir

Rio Grande
Río Bravo del Norte

Amistad
Reservoir

Chihuahua
Desert

MAPIMÍ
BASIN

CABALLOS
MESTEÑOS
PLAIN

Balsas River

Lerma
River

Lake
Chapala

SIERRA MADRE DEL SUR

Infiernillo
Reservoir

Petacalco
Bay

Point
Tejupan

Rio Grande
de Santiago

SIERRA MADRE OCCIDENTAL

San Pedro R.

Conchos R.

Point Mita
Banderas Bay
Cape
Corrientes

Marías Is.

400 mi

400 km

200

200

0

0

Bavispe R.

Álvaro
Obregón
Reservoir

Copper
Canyon

Fuerte R.

Yaqui R.

Sonora
River

Sonoran
Desert

Altar
Desert

Colorado
River

SIERRA
SAN PEDRO
MÁRTIR

Laguna Salada
33 ft. (10 m)
below sea level

Tiburón I.

Angel de la
Guarda I.

Gulf of California

Baja

California

Cerralvo I.

Cape
San Lucas

Cape San Lázaro

Magdalena I.
Magdalena Bay

Vizcaíno
Desert

Cedros I.
Sebastián Vizcaíno
Bay

Eugenia
Point

San Antonio
Point

Guadalupe I.

Revillagigedo Islands

PACIFIC
OCEAN

N
E
W S

TROPIC OF CANCER

77

South America

Caribbean Sea

Legend
- International boundary
- ⊛ National capital
- ★ Other capital

Symbol and label sizes indicate relative sizes of cities:
- ● **Rio de Janeiro**
- • Santos
- · Jataí

Facts

- Area: 6,900,000 square miles (17,800,000 square kilometers)
- Highest Point: Mt. Aconcagua, Argentina, 22,834 ft (6,960 m)
- Lowest Point: Valdés Peninsula, Argentina, 131 ft (40 m) below sea level
- Longest River: Amazon, 4,000 mi (6,400 km)
- Largest Lake: Lake Titicaca, Peru/Bolivia, 3,200 sq. mi (8,300 sq. km)
- Largest Country: Brazil, 6,880,000 sq. mi (17,819,000 sq. km) (slightly smaller than the United States)
- Largest City: São Paulo, Brazil, 17,834,000

NORTH AMERICA

Caribbean Sea

Gulf of Panama

Galápagos Islands

Pariñas Pt.

Gulf of Guayaquil

PACIFIC OCEAN

Lake Maracaibo

LLANOS

Cauca River

Magdalena River

Orinoco River

Angel Falls ≈

GUIANA HIGHLANDS

Orinoco River

Rio Negro

AMAZON BASIN

Putumayo River

Amazon (Solimões) River

Marañón River

Ucayali River

Juruá River

Purus River

Madeira River

Amazon River

Tapajós River

Teles Pires River

Xingu River

River

Araguaia River

Tocantins River

Parnaíba River

São Francisco River

BRAZILIAN HIGHLANDS

Mt. Huascarán 22,133 ft. (6,746 m) ▲

Paracas Peninsula

Volcán Misti 19,098 ft. (5,821 m) ▲

Lake Titicaca

Mt. Illimani 20,741 ft. (6,322 m) ▲

Lake Poopó

ALTIPLANO

Atacama Desert

ANDES

Guaporé River

MATO GROSSO PLATEAU

Beni River

Mamoré River

GRAN CHACO

Pilcomayo River

Paraguay River

Paraná River

Grande River

SERRA DO MAR

Iguazú Falls

Salado River

Paraná River

Uruguay River

San Félix I.   San Ambrosio I.

Juan Fernández Is.

Mt. Aconcagua 22,834 ft. (6,960 m) ▲

PAMPAS

Río de la Plata

ATLANTIC OCEAN

Chiloé I.

Colorado River

Negro River

Gulf of San Matías

▽ Valdés Peninsula 131 ft (40 m) below sea level

Los Chonos Archipelago

Patagonia

Gulf of San Jorge

Santa Cruz River

Strait of Magellan

Tierra del Fuego

Cape Horn

Falkland Islands (Islas Malvinas)

South Georgia

Cape São Roque

ATLANTIC OCEAN

EQUATOR

TROPIC OF CAPRICORN

TROPIC OF CAPRICORN

ANDES

ANDES

90°W   80°W   70°W   60°W   50°W   40°W

100°W   90°W   80°W   70°W   60°W   50°W   40°W   30°W   20°W

10°N   EQUATOR   10°S   20°S   30°S   40°S   50°S

Elevation Profile

Legend	
International boundary	
▲ Mountain peak	
▽ Lowest point	
≈ Falls	

Scale:
0   300   600 mi
0   300   600 km

N
W   E
S

ARCTIC OCEAN
NORTH AMERICA   EUROPE   ASIA
ATLANTIC OCEAN   AFRICA   PACIFIC OCEAN
PACIFIC OCEAN   SOUTH AMERICA   INDIAN OCEAN   AUSTRALIA
Equator
ANTARCTICA
Robinson Projection

Elevation Profile labels:
Paracas Peninsula   Lake Titicaca   Andes Mountains   Mato Grosso Plateau   Brazilian Highlands
20,000 ft.
10,000 ft.
5,000 ft.
Sea level
A   B

Major Metropolitan Areas

Argentina
Buenos Aires	11,298,000
Córdoba	1,209,000
Rosario	1,119,000

Bolivia
La Paz	1,484,000
Santa Cruz	1,136,000
Cochabamba	517,000

Brazil
São Paulo	17,834,000
Rio de Janeiro	10,612,000
Belo Horizonte	4,800,000
Pôrto Alegre	3,655,000
Recife	3,332,000
Salvador	3,018,000
Fortaleza	2,975,000
Brasília	2,942,000
Curitiba	2,726,000
Belém	1,816,000
Manaus	1,011,000

Chile
Santiago	4,647,000
Viña del Mar	299,000

Colombia
Bogotá	6,422,000
Cali	2,129,000
Medellín	1,885,000
Barranquilla	1,549,000

Ecuador
Guayaquil	2,118,000
Quito	1,616,000

French Guiana
Cayenne	50,000

Guyana
Georgetown	187,000

Paraguay
Asunción	513,000

Peru
Lima	6,988,000
Arequipa	830,000
Chiclayo	766,000

Suriname
Paramaribo	291,000

Uruguay
Montevideo	1,303,000

Venezuela
Caracas	3,061,000
Maracaibo	1,220,000
Barquisimeto	896,000
Valencia	742,000

International comparability of population data is limited by varying census methods. Where metropolitan population is unavailable, core city population is shown.

Population

Persons per sq. mile	Persons per sq. km
Over 520	Over 200
260 to 519	100 to 199
130 to 259	50 to 99
25 to 129	10 to 49
1 to 24	1 to 9
0	0

Major metropolitan areas
- ● Over 2 million
- ● 1 million to 2 million
- • Under 1 million

Estimated 2002 Population (in millions)

- Brazil 172
- Colombia 39
- Argentina 37
- Peru 27
- Venezuela 23
- Chile 15
- Ecuador 13
- Bolivia 8
- Paraguay 5
- All other countries 4

Source: U.S. Census Bureau

Electricity Use

United States 12,407

Suriname 4,150

Chile 2,311

Columbia 1,005

Paraguay 334

KWh (kilowatt hours) per person per year

Source: *World Factbook*, CIA, 2001

Gross Domestic Product

GDP per capita

- Over $20,000
- $10,000 to $20,000
- $5,000 to $9,999
- $2,500 to $4,999
- Less than $2,500
- No data

Source: *World Factbook*, CIA, 2001

Gross Domestic Product is a measure of the total goods and services generated by a country. Generally, manufacturing, high-tech services, and specialized agricultural products add more value than raw materials and basic food stuffs.

Non-manufacturing economic activity is generated primarily by commercial plantation agriculture, livestock raising, and the harvest of forest products, plus the extraction of oil and minerals. Manufacturing, like population, is concentrated in the continent's coastal areas.

Land Use and Resources

Predominant land use

- Commercial agriculture
- Livestock ranching
- Subsistence agriculture
- Primarily forestland
- Limited agricultural activity

Major resources

- Coal
- Natural gas
- Oil
- Forest products
- Gold (Au)
- Silver (Ag)
- Iron ore (Fe)

- Uranium (U)
- Bauxite (Al)
- Diamonds
- Other minerals
- Fishing
- Major manufacturing and trade centers

Most of the continent is under the influence of wet and tropical air. Warm currents in the Atlantic Ocean as well as wet lowland elevations lying within the confines of the tropical latitudes directly affect the climate of the majority of the land area. The Andes Mountains and cold currents that hug the Pacific coast keep the Western and Southern regions of the continent temperate but dry.

See photographs taken in different kinds of climates on pages 24–25.

Rivadavia
Highest recorded temperature 120°F (49°C)

Sarmiento
Lowest recorded temperature -27°F (-33°C)

Climate

- Tropical wet
- Tropical wet and dry
- Arid
- Semiarid
- Mediterranean
- Humid subtropical
- Marine
- Subarctic
- Highland

Quibdo
Highest average annual precipitation: 354" (899 cm)

Arica
Lowest average annual precipitation: 0.03" (0.08 cm)

Moist and unstable air above the Equator—as well as highlands that wring out waterlogged clouds—produce heavy rainfall, but along the coast of Chile and elsewhere, cold ocean water and mountainous barriers keep rainfall at a minimum.

Annual Precipitation

Centimeters	Inches
Over 200	Over 80
150 to 200	60 to 80
100 to 150	40 to 60
50 to 100	20 to 40
25 to 50	10 to 20
Under 25	Under 10

Climate Graphs

Average daily temperature range (in °F) — High / Low
Average monthly precipitation (in inches)

100°
65°
32°
0°

20°
10°
0°

ASUNCIÓN, Paraguay

BOGOTÁ, Colombia

BUENOS AIRES, Argentina

CARACAS, Venezuela

CAYENNE, French Guiana

LA PAZ, Bolivia

LIMA, Peru

MANAUS, Brazil

PUNTA ARENAS, Chile

RECIFE, Brazil

RIO DE JANEIRO, Brazil

SANTIAGO, Chile

South America is dominated by tropical vegetation, including Earth's most extensive rain forest. Farther south, a vast grassland, the Pampa, fades gradually into the dry and meager vegetation of Patagonia.
See photographs of the different kinds of vegetation on pages 26–27.

Vegetation

- Unclassified highlands or ice cap
- Midlatitude deciduous forest
- Mixed forest
- Midlatitude scrubland
- Midlatitude grassland
- Desert
- Tropical seasonal and scrub
- Tropical rain forest
- Tropical savanna

The destruction of forest areas—especially in the Amazon Basin—is one of the leading environmental issues in South America. In Brazil, it is estimated that an average of 15,000 acres of forest are lost each day as people clear land for timber and to grow crops. Human activities have impacted other types of vegetation, as well. For example, over-grazing has caused damage to grasslands in many areas, putting them at risk of becoming infertile deserts. Poor urban air quality is another serious concern in the region, with nearly 80 percent of the population living in cities.

Environmental Issues

- Current forest
- Cleared forest
- Area at highest risk of desertification
- ● Poor air quality*

*Cities exceeding at least one of the World Health Organization's (WHO) annual mean guidelines for air quality

Sources: *Global Distribution of Original and Remaining Forests*, UNEP-WCMC, 2002
World Soil Resources Map Index, USDA/NRCS, 2002
World Development Indicators, World Bank, 1999

Europe

Facts

- Area: 4,032,000 square mi. (10,443,000 square kilometers)
- Highest Point: Mt. Elbrus, Russia, 18,510 ft. (5,642 m)
- Lowest Point: Caspian Sea 92 ft. (28 m) below sea level
- Longest River: Volga, 2,290 mi. (3,685 km)
- Largest Lake: Caspian Sea, 143,244 sq. mi. (371,000 sq. km)
- Largest Country: Russia (European), 1,663,870 sq. mi. (4,309,400 sq. km)
- Largest City: Paris, France 9,645,000 (metropolitan pop.)

International boundary
⊛ National capital
★ Other capital

Symbol and label sizes indicate relative sizes of cities:
● **London**
● Helsinki
· Varna

ASIA

ASIA

AFRICA

Caspian Sea
92 ft. (28 m)
below sea level

Caspian Depression   Caspian Sea

Sea of Azov

Black Sea   Black Sea

Carpathian Mountains

Massif Central   Mt. Blanc   Alps

Elevation Profile

International boundary
Canal
▲ Mountain peak
▽ Lowest point

15,000 ft.
10,000 ft.
5,000 ft.
Sea level

ATLANTIC
OCEAN

500 mi
500 km
0   250
0   250   500

Major Metropolitan Areas

Albania
Tirana — 244,000

Andorra
Andorra la Vella — 21,000

Armenia
Yerevan — 1,247,000

Austria
Vienna — 1,562,000

Azerbaijan
Baku — 1,792,000

Belarus
Minsk — 1,681,000

Belgium
Brussels — 978,000
Antwerp — 449,000

Bosnia & Herzegovina
Sarajevo — 529,000

Bulgaria
Sofia — 1,191,000

Croatia
Zagreb — 692,000

Czech Republic
Prague — 1,179,000

Denmark
Copenhagen — 1,085,000

Estonia
Tallinn — 398,000

Finland
Helsinki — 965,000

France
Paris — 9,645,000
Marseille — 1,350,000
Lyon — 1,349,000
Lille — 1,001,000

Georgia
Tbilisi — 1,399,000

Germany (core city only)
Berlin — 3,382,000
Hamburg — 1,715,000
Munich — 1,210,000
Cologne — 963,000
Frankfurt — 647,000
Essen — 595,000
Dortmund — 589,000
Stuttgart — 584,000
Düsseldorf — 569,000

Greece
Athens — 3,073,000

Hungary
Budapest — 1,825,000

Iceland
Reykjavík — 175,000

Ireland
Dublin — 1,123,000

Italy
Rome — 2,460,000
Milan — 1,183,000
Naples — 993,000
Turin — 857,000
Palermo — 653,000
Genoa — 604,000

Latvia
Riga — 793,000

Liechtenstein
Vaduz — 5,000

Lithuania
Vilnius — 578,000

Luxembourg
Luxembourg — 77,000

F.Y.R. Macedonia
Skopje — 545,000

Malta
Valletta — 8,000

Moldova
Chişinău — 658,000

Monaco
Monaco — 27,000

Netherlands
Amsterdam — 1,207,000
Rotterdam — 1,161,000

Norway
Oslo — 513,000

Poland
Warsaw — 1,610,000
Łódź — 787,000
Kraków — 741,000
Wrocław — 634,000

Portugal
Lisbon — 1,947,000

Romania
Bucharest — 2,009,000

Russia (European)
Moscow — 8,538,000
St. Petersburg — 4,678,000
Niżnij Novgorod — 1,366,000
Samara — 1,183,000
Kazan' — 1,092,000
Ufa — 1,094,000
Volgograd — 1,025,000
Perm' — 1,024,000
Rostov-na-Donu — 1,004,000

San Marino
San Marino — 5,000

Serbia & Montenegro
Belgrade — 1,619,000

Slovakia
Bratislava — 429,000

Slovenia
Ljubljana — 264,000

Spain
Madrid — 2,939,000
Barcelona — 1,504,000
Valencia — 738,000
Seville — 685,000

Sweden
Stockholm — 1,665,000

Switzerland
Zürich — 933,000
Geneva — 451,000

Turkey (European)
Istanbul — 8,803,000

Ukraine
Kiev — 2,590,000
Kharkiv — 1,494,000
Dnipropetrovs'k — 1,109,000
Donets'k — 1,050,000
Odesa — 1,002,000

United Kingdom
London — 7,652,000
Birmingham — 2,296,000
Manchester — 2,277,000
Leeds-Bradford — 1,446,000
Newcastle — 886,000
Glasgow — 867,000
Liverpool — 838,000
Sheffield — 633,000

International comparability of population data is limited by varying census methods. Where metropolitan population is unavailable, core city population is shown.

Population

Persons per sq. mile	Persons per sq. km	Major metropolitan areas
Over 520	Over 200	● Over 2 million
260 to 519	100 to 199	• 1 million to 2 million
130 to 259	50 to 99	· Under 1 million
25 to 129	10 to 49	
1 to 24	1 to 9	
0	0	

Estimated 2002 Population (in millions)

Russia 145
Germany 83
United Kingdom 60
France 60
Italy 58
Ukraine 48
Spain 40
Poland 39
Romania 22
All other countries 365

Source: U.S. Census Bureau

Gross Domestic Product

GDP per capita

- Over $20,000
- $10,000 to $20,000
- $5,000 to $9,999
- $2,500 to $4,999
- Under $2,500
- No data

Source: *World Factbook*, CIA, 2001

Gross Domestic Product is a measure of the total goods and services generated by a country. Generally, manufacturing, high-tech services, and specialized agricultural products add more value than raw materials and basic food stuffs.

Electricity Use

- Iceland 23,655
- Finland 15,768
- United States 12,407
- France 6,696
- Germany 5,964
- United Kingdom 5,583
- Moldova 1,304

KWh (kilowatt hours) per person per year

Source: *World Factbook*, CIA, 2001

Land Use and Resources

Predominant land use

- Commercial agriculture
- Dairying
- Livestock ranching
- Nomadic herding
- Subsistence agriculture
- Primarily forestland
- Limited agricultural activity

Major resources

- Coal
- Natural gas
- Oil
- Au Gold
- Fe Iron ore
- Ag Silver
- U Uranium
- Al Bauxite
- Other minerals
- Fishing
- Major manufacturing and trade centers

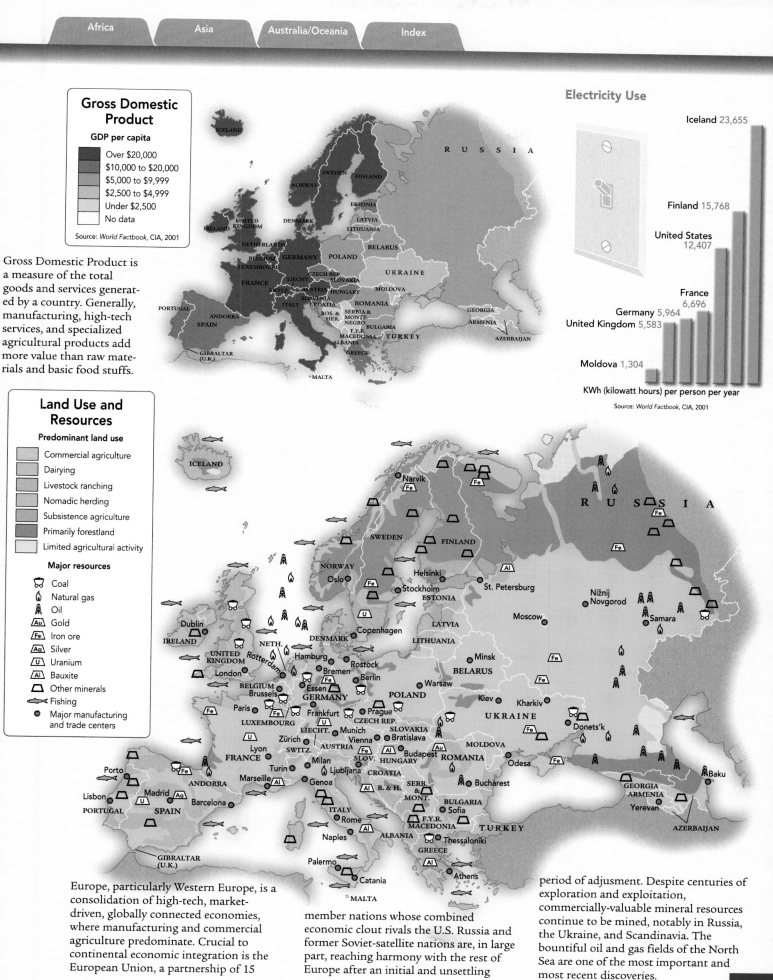

Europe, particularly Western Europe, is a consolidation of high-tech, market-driven, globally connected economies, where manufacturing and commercial agriculture predominate. Crucial to continental economic integration is the European Union, a partnership of 15 member nations whose combined economic clout rivals the U.S. Russia and former Soviet-satellite nations are, in large part, reaching harmony with the rest of Europe after an initial and unsettling period of adjustment. Despite centuries of exploration and exploitation, commercially-valuable mineral resources continue to be mined, notably in Russia, the Ukraine, and Scandinavia. The bountiful oil and gas fields of the North Sea are one of the most important and most recent discoveries.

Climate

- Semiarid
- Mediterranean
- Humid subtropical
- Marine
- Humid continental
- Subarctic
- Tundra
- Ice cap
- Highland

The far-reaching influence and effects of warm ocean currents cannot be overstated. The ceaseless torrent distributed by the Gulf Stream along the coasts of Western Europe, even to the shores of Iceland and Norway, produces much milder weather than would be expected at its latitudes and provides a ready source of moisture. Along the Mediterranean margin of Europe the typical weather—mild, wet winters and hot, dry summers—has been defined as a climate category that is now used worldwide.

See photographs taken in different kinds of climates on pages 24–25.

Annual Precipitation

Centimeters	Inches
Over 200	Over 80
150 to 200	60 to 80
100 to 150	40 to 60
50 to 100	20 to 40
25 to 50	10 to 20
Under 25	Under 10

Though regionally formidable mountains rise to extract snow and rain, no continental-scale alpine barrier exists—thereby permitting moisture-laden, westerly winds springing from warm oceanic waters to distribute precipitation uniformly across Europe. However, by the time these currents of air reach the landlocked heart of Eastern Europe, northeast of the Black Sea, much of the moisture has already been spent.

Climate Graphs

Average daily temperature range (in °F) | Average monthly precipitation (in inches)

High | Low

ARKHANGELSK, Russia

ATHENS, Greece

COPENHAGEN, Denmark

DUBLIN, Ireland

LISBON, Portugal

MOSCOW, Russia

NAPLES, Italy

ODESA, Ukraine

PARIS, France

REYKJAVÍK, Iceland

TROMSØ, Norway

VIENNA, Austria

Vegetation

- Unclassified highlands or ice cap
- Tundra and alpine tundra
- Coniferous forest
- Midlatitude deciduous forest
- Mixed forest
- Midlatitude scrubland
- Midlatitude grassland

Forests, nourished by plentiful precipitation, dominate in Europe, but grassland and scrubland thrive where rainfall becomes sparse or is seasonal. Deciduous trees disappear as the winters grow harsh, replaced by vast and hardy stands of coniferous forest that are merely the western end of an immense belt stretching across Russia to the Pacific Ocean.

See photographs of the different kinds of vegetation on pages 26–27.

Environmental Issues

- Current forest
- Cleared forest
- Area at highest risk of desertification
- Areas most affected by acid rain
- Poor air quality*

*Cities exceeding at least one of the World Health Organization's (WHO) annual mean guidelines for air quality

Sources: Global Distribution of Original and Remaining Forests, UNEP-WCMC, 2002
World Soil Resources Map Index, USDA/NRCS, 2002
World Development Indicators, World Bank, 1999

Emissions from the many cars, trucks, and factories in Europe have led to problems with air pollution and acid rain over a large part of the continent. Land and water pollution (from fertilizers, pesticides, and industrial waste) is also widespread. Since the 1960's, the amount of forest area in Western and Central Europe has actually increased, but many forests (nearly 60%) are damaged due to acidification, pollution, drought, or fires. Overfishing—especially in the North Sea—is a serious problem for marine ecosystems.

Africa

Legend
- International boundary
- ⊛ National capital
- ★ Other capital

Symbol and label sizes indicate relative sizes of cities:
- ● **Johannesburg**
- ● Dar es Salaam
- · Malabo

Facts

- Area: 11,677,239 square miles (30,244,049 square kilometers)
- Highest Point: Mt. Kilimanjaro, Tanzania 19,340 ft. (5,895 m)
- Lowest Point: Lake Assal, Djibouti 512 ft. (156 m) below sea level
- Longest River: Nile 4,160 mi. (6,695 km)
- Largest Lake: Lake Victoria, Uganda/Kenya/ Tanzania 26,828 sq. mi. (69,484 sq. km)
- Largest Country: Sudan 967,500 sq. mi. (2,505,813 sq. km)
- Largest City: Cairo, Egypt 6,801,000

Legend

	International boundary
▲	Mountain peak
▽	Lowest point
≈	Falls

EUROPE

Mediterranean Sea

ASIA

ATLANTIC OCEAN

INDIAN OCEAN

Strait of Gibraltar

Madeira Is.

Canary Is.

Cape Bojador

Cape Blanc

Cape Verde Islands

Cap Vert

ATLAS MTS.

▲ Jebel Toubkal 13,665 ft. (4,165 m)

Grand Erg Occidental

Grand Erg Oriental

TADEMAÏT PLATEAU

Erg Chech

Tahat 9,573 ft. (2,918 m) ▲

AHAGGAR MTS.

S A H A R A

AÏR MTS.

Ténéré

Tibesti Mts.

▲ Emi Koussi 11,204 ft. (3,415 m)

MARRA MTS.

Gulf of Gabes

Gulf of Sidra

Tripolitania

Cyrenaica

Libyan Desert

Nile Delta

Suez Canal

Sinai Peninsula

Gulf of Aqaba

Gulf of Suez

Qattara Depression

Eastern Desert

Nile R.

Lake Nasser

Nubian Desert

Red Sea

Bab al Mandab

Gulf of Aden

Cape Gwardafuy

TROPIC OF CANCER

Ras Dashen 15,157 ft. (4,620 m)

Denakil

▽ Lake Assal 512 ft. (156 m) below sea level

Somali Peninsula

Horn of Africa

Ogaden

Lake Tana

Blue Nile

White Nile

ETHIOPIAN HIGHLANDS

Senegal River

Niger

Lake Chad

S A H E L

Jos Plateau

Chari R.

Benue R.

Niger River

Lake Volta

Grain Coast

Ivory Coast

Gold Coast

Slave Coast

Bight of Benin

Niger Delta

Gulf of Guinea

ADAMAWA MTS.

▲ Cameroon Mtn. 13,451 ft. (4,100 m)

Bioko

Principe

São Tomé

Annobón

Cape Lopez

EQUATOR

Ubangi

Congo River

CONGO BASIN

Kasai

Lualaba River

Lomami River

Margherita Pk. 16,762 ft. (5,109 m) ▲

RUWENZORI MTS.

Lake Albert

Lake Kivu

Lake Victoria

Rift Valley

▲ Mt. Kenya 17,057 ft. (5,199 m)

Lake Turkana

Webi Jubba

Sudd

KATANGA PLATEAU

MITUMBA MTS.

Lake Tanganyika

Lake Mweru

Rift Valley

▲ Mt. Kilimanjaro 19,340 ft. (5,895 m)

Pemba I.

Zanzibar I.

Cape Delgado

Seychelles Is.

BIÉ PLATEAU

Cubango R.

Cuando

Lake Nyasa (Lake Malawi)

MUCHINGA MTS.

Ruvuma R.

Comoros Is.

Cap d'Ambre

Ascension

St. Helena

Cape Fria

Skeleton Coast

Namib Desert

Damaraland

Kalahari Desert

Okavango

L. Kariba

Zambezi R.

Victoria Falls

Limpopo R.

Orange R.

Vaal

R.

Barra Point

Mozambique Channel

Madagascar

BEMARAHA PLATEAU

Mauritius

Reunion

Cap Ste. Marie

TROPIC OF CAPRICORN

▲ Thabana Ntlenyana 11,425 ft. (3,482 m)

DRAKENSBERG

Cape of Good Hope

Cape Agulhas

Scale:
0 — 500 — 1,000 mi
0 — 500 — 1,000 km

ARCTIC OCEAN

NORTH AMERICA

EUROPE

ASIA

ATLANTIC OCEAN

AFRICA

PACIFIC OCEAN

Equator

SOUTH AMERICA

PACIFIC OCEAN

INDIAN OCEAN

AUSTRALIA

ANTARCTICA

Robinson Projection

Elevation Profile

Jebel Toubkal	Ahaggar Mountains	Sahara	Sahel		Lake Victoria		Great	Mt. Kilimanjaro
					Nile River		Rift	
					Great Rift Valley,		Valley	
					Lake Albert			

20,000 ft.
10,000 ft.
5,000 ft.
Sea level A — B

Major Metropolitan Areas

Algeria
Algiers — 1,904,000 (metro)
Oran — 745,000
Constantine — 564,000

Angola
Luanda — 1,822,000

Benin
Cotonou — 537,000
Porto-Novo — 179,000

Botswana
Gaborone — 186,000

Burkina Faso
Ouagadougou — 634,000

Burundi
Bujumbura — 234,000

Cameroon
Douala — 810,000
Yaoundé — 649,000

Cape Verde
Praia — 103,000

Central African Republic
Bangui — 452,000

Chad
N'Djamena — 547,000

Comoros
Moroni — 30,000

Congo, Democratic Republic of the
Kinshasa — 4,657,000
Lubumbashi — 565,000

Congo, Republic of the
Brazzaville — 596,000

Côte d'Ivoire
Abidjan — 1,929,000
Yamoussoukro — 107,000

Djibouti
Djibouti — 62,000

Egypt
Cairo — 6,801,000
Alexandria — 3,339,000
Giza — 2,222,000

Equatorial Guinea
Malabo — 30,000

Eritrea
Asmara — 358,000

Ethiopia
Addis Ababa — 2,424,000

Gabon
Libreville — 420,000

The Gambia
Banjul — 271,000

Ghana
Accra — 1,155,000

Guinea
Conakry — 705,000

Guinea-Bissau
Bissau — 109,000

Kenya
Nairobi — 2,143,000
Mombasa — 465,000

Lesotho
Maseru — 138,000

Liberia
Monrovia — 421,000

Libya
Tripoli — 1,500,000

Madagascar
Antananarivo — 1,103,000

Malawi
Blantyre — 502,000
Lilongwe — 440,000

Mali
Bamako — 1,179,000

Mauritania
Nouakchott — 612,000

Mauritius
Port Louis — 128,000

Morocco
Casablanca — 2,943,000
Rabat — 1,220,000
Marrakesh — 602,000

Mozambique
Maputo — 989,000

Namibia
Windhoek — 147,000

Niger
Niamey — 397,000

Nigeria
Lagos — 5,195,000
Kano — 2,167,000
Ibadan — 1,835,000

Rwanda
Kigali — 234,000

São Tomé & Príncipe
São Tomé — 6,000

Senegal
Dakar — 1,977,000

Seychelles
Victoria — 25,000

Sierra Leone
Freetown — 470,000

Somalia
Mogadishu — 230,000

South Africa
Durban — 2,992,000
Cape Town — 2,898,000
Johannesburg — 2,885,000
Pretoria — 2,086,000
Port Elizabeth — 1,312,000

Sudan
Omdurman — 1,271,000
Khartoum — 947,000

Swaziland
Mbabane — 38,000

Tanzania
Dar es Salaam — 1,361,000

Togo
Lomé — 450,000

Tunisia
Tunis — 674,000

Uganda
Kampala — 1,209,000

Western Sahara
el-Aaiún — 90,000

Zambia
Lusaka — 1,270,000

Zimbabwe
Harare — 1,189,000

International comparability of population data is limited by varying census methods. Where metropolitan population is unavailable, core city population is shown.

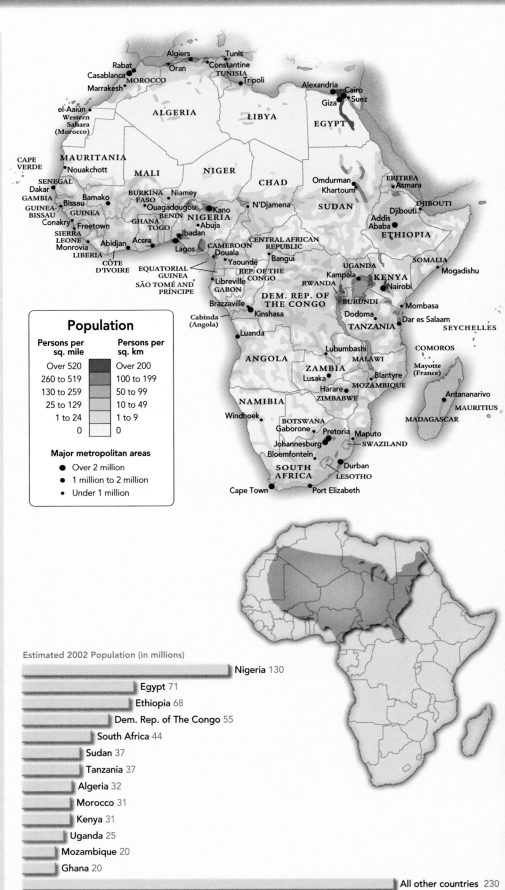

Population

Persons per sq. mile		Persons per sq. km
Over 520		Over 200
260 to 519		100 to 199
130 to 259		50 to 99
25 to 129		10 to 49
1 to 24		1 to 9
0		0

Major metropolitan areas
- ● Over 2 million
- ● 1 million to 2 million
- • Under 1 million

Estimated 2002 Population (in millions)

Nigeria 130
Egypt 71
Ethiopia 68
Dem. Rep. of The Congo 55
South Africa 44
Sudan 37
Tanzania 37
Algeria 32
Morocco 31
Kenya 31
Uganda 25
Mozambique 20
Ghana 20
All other countries 230

Source: U.S. Census Bureau

Gross Domestic Product is a measure of the total goods and services generated by a country. Generally, manufacturing, high-tech services, and specialized agricultural products add more value than raw materials and basic food stuffs.

South Africa is the only African nation considered to have a developed economy, even though their GDP is less then half that of the United States.

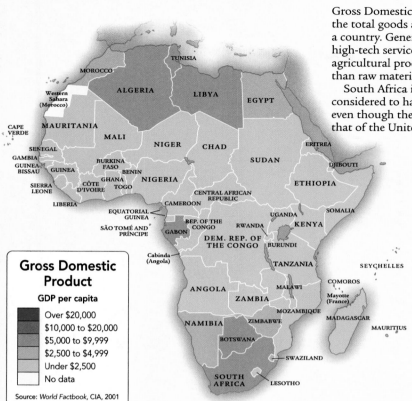

Gross Domestic Product

GDP per capita

- Over $20,000
- $10,000 to $20,000
- $5,000 to $9,999
- $2,500 to $4,999
- Under $2,500
- No data

Source: *World Factbook*, CIA, 2001

Electricity Use

United States 12,407

South Africa 3,955

Seychelles 1,867

Namibia 1,084

Zimbabwe 611

Cameroon 204

KWh (kilowatt hours) per person per year

Source: *World Factbook*, CIA, 2001

Agriculture supplies the livelihood for the vast majority of Africans. Agricultural exports include coffee, cocoa beans, peanuts, palm oil, and spices. These important export crops are mainly cultivated on plantations and large farms. Areas of subsistence farming supply the needs of local communities.

Unfortunately, poor soils and unfavorable climate conditions, as well as political unrest and unstable economies, all have an adverse impact on agricultural activity and therefore the standard of living.

Minerals account for more then one half of Africa's exports. Oil, diamonds, gold, cobalt, and several other minerals are leading exports. However, important mineral deposits are limited to a handful of countries.

Manufacturing has been slow to develop on the continent. Lack of money and skilled labor are the main deterrents.

Land Use and Resources

Predominant land use

- Commercial agriculture
- Livestock ranching
- Subsistence agriculture
- Nomadic herding
- Primarily forestland
- Limited agricultural activity

Major resources

- Coal
- Natural gas
- Oil
- Au Gold
- Fe Iron ore
- Pt Platinum
- U Uranium
- Al Bauxite
- Diamonds
- Other minerals
- Fishing
- Major manufacturing and trade centers

The climate of Africa is clearly a study in geographic contrasts. Perpetually wet and tropical areas surrounding the Equator quickly acquire seasonal variety as you move north and south. Roaming even farther leads to the vast, hot and arid zones of northern and southern Africa. The influence of neighboring water bodies is limited to small regions of northern Africa, namely Morocco, Algeria, and Libya, where the mild currents of the Mediterranean Sea temper the climate, and eastern South Africa, where the mixture of warm currents flowing close to shore and the seasonal onshore winds striking the Drakensberg uplands provide for a moist and temperate marine coast climate.

See photographs taken in different kinds of climates on pages 24–25.

Climate

- Tropical wet
- Tropical wet and dry
- Arid
- Semiarid
- Mediterranean
- Humid subtropical
- Marine
- Highland

Ifrane
Lowest recorded temperature, -11°F (-24°C)

El Azizia
Highest recorded temperature, 136°F (58°C)

Wadi Halfa
Lowest average annual precipitation: 0.1" (0.254 cm)

Debundscha
Highest average annual precipitation: 405" (1,029 cm)

Annual Precipitation

Centimeters	Inches
Over 203	Over 80
152 to 203	60 to 80
102 to 152	40 to 60
51 to 102	20 to 40
25 to 51	10 to 20
Under 25	Under 10

Africa's precipitation pattern is determined by its position on Earth's grid. Heavy precipitation near the Equator dwindles both to north, home of the immense Sahara, and to the south, realm of the Namib and Kalahari Deserts. Moist conditions exist on Madagascar as a result of the tropical influences of winds and currents from the Indian Ocean.

Climate Graphs

Average daily temperature range (in °F) — High, Low
Average monthly precipitation (in inches)

ADDIS ABABA, Ethiopia

ANTANANARIVO, Madagascar

CAIRO, Egypt

CAPE TOWN, South Africa

CASABLANCA, Morocco

CONAKRY, Guinea

DAKAR, Senegal

DAR ES SALAAM, Tanzania

FAYA-LARGEAU, Chad

KINSHASA, Dem. Rep. of the Congo

LAGOS, Nigeria

LUSAKA, Zambia

The dense, tropical rain forest surrounding the Equator is offset by the contrastingly sparse vegetation on the rest of the continent. Vast areas consist of grassland and scrub vegetation with trees only occasionally dotting the landscape. Evergreen and mixed forests of more temperate climates are limited to the Mediterranean areas of Morocco and Algeria, the Ethiopian Highlands, and Kenya.

See photographs of the different kinds of vegetation on pages 26–27.

Vegetation

- Coniferous forest
- Mixed forest
- Midlatitude scrubland
- Midlatitude grassland
- Desert
- Tropical seasonal and scrub
- Tropical rain forest
- Tropical savanna

Environmental Issues

- Current forest
- Cleared forest
- Area at highest risk of desertification
- ● Poor air quality*

*Cities exceeding at least one of the World Health Organization's (WHO) annual mean guidelines for air quality

Sources: *Global Distribution of Original and Remaining Forests,* UNEP-WCMC, 2002
World Soil Resources Map Index, USDA/NRCS, 2002
World Development Indicators, World Bank, 1999

Desertification (land turning into desert) is one of the leading environmental issues in Africa. Two leading causes of desertification are the removal of vegetation (often for cooking fuel) and overgrazing, especially in semiarid and drought-prone areas. Other environmental problems include deforestation, soil loss, declining biodiversity, and decreasing air and water quality. Water scarcity is also a concern in many African countries, such as Egypt, Libya, Algeria, Tunisia, and Morocco.

Asia

- Area: 17,139,000 square miles (44,390,000 square kilometers)
- Highest Point: Mt. Everest, China/Nepal 29,035 ft. (8,850 m)
- Lowest Point: Dead Sea, Israel/Jordan 1,310 ft. (399 m) below sea level
- Longest River: Chang (Yangtze), China 3,964 mi. (6,379 km)
- Largest Lake: Caspian Sea 143,244 sq. mi. (371,000 sq. km)
- Largest Country: Russia (Asian) 4,928,980 sq. mi. (12,766,000 sq. km)
- Largest City: Mumbai, India 16,368,000

International boundary

⊛ National capital

★ Other capital

Symbol and label sizes indicate relative sizes of cities:

● **Bangalore**

• Chengdu

· Magadan

96

Major Metropolitan Areas

Afghanistan
Kabul — 2,029,000

Bahrain
Manama — 151,000

Bangladesh
Dhaka — 6,487,000

Bhutan
Thimphu — 8,900

Brunei
Bandar Seri Begawan — 50,000

Cambodia
Phnom Penh — 1,000,000

China
Shanghai — 12,910,000
Beijing — 10,820,000
Tianjin — 8,970,000
Hong Kong — 6,708,000
Shenyang — 4,740,000
Wuhan — 4,450,000
Chongqing — 4,070,000
Guangzhou — 3,910,000
Chengdu — 3,120,000
Xi'an — 2,990,000
Harbin — 2,960,000
Nanjing — 2,670,000

Cyprus
Nicosia — 273,000

East Timor
Dili — 140,000

India
Mumbai (Bombay) — 16,368,000
Kolkata (Calcutta) — 13,217,000
Delhi — 12,791,000
Chennai (Madras) — 6,425,000
Bangalore — 5,687,000
Hyderabad — 5,534,000

Indonesia
Jakarta — 9,374,000
Bandung — 5,919,000
Bogor — 5,000,000
Malang — 3,174,000

Iran
Tehran — 6,759,000
Mashhad — 1,887,000

Iraq
Baghdad — 4,336,000

Israel
Tel Aviv-Jaffa — 2,595,000
Jerusalem — 628,000

Japan
Tokyo — 12,059,000
Yokohama — 3,427,000
Osaka — 2,599,000
Nagoya — 2,171,000
Sapporo — 1,822,000
Kobe — 1,494,000
Kyoto — 1,468,000
Fukuoka — 1,341,000
Kawasaki — 1,250,000
Hiroshima — 1,126,000

Jordan
Amman — 1,147,000

Kazakhstan
Almaty — 1,129,000

North Korea
P'yŏngyang — 2,741,000

South Korea (core city only)
Seoul — 9,854,000
Busan — 3,655,000
Daegu — 2,474,000

Kuwait
Kuwait — 193,000

Kyrgyzstan
Bishkek — 753,000

Population

Persons per sq. mile		Persons per sq. km	
Over 520		Over 200	
260 to 519		100 to 199	
130 to 259		50 to 99	
25 to 129		10 to 49	
1 to 24		1 to 9	
0		0	

Major metropolitan areas
● Over 2 million
● 1 million to 2 million
• Under 1 million

Estimated 2002 Population (in millions)

China 1,284
India 1,046
Indonesia 232
Pakistan 148
Bangladesh 133
Japan 127
Philippines 85
Vietnam 81
Turkey 67
Iran 67
Thailand 62
South Korea 48
All other countries 365

Source: U.S. Census Bueau

Laos
Vientiane — 331,000

Lebanon
Beirut — 1,500,000

Malaysia
Kuala Lumpur — 1,379,000

Maldives
Male — 74,000

Mongolia
Ulaanbaatar — 760,000

Myanmar (Burma)
Yangon (Rangoon) — 4,101,000

Nepal
Kathmandu — 421,000

Oman
Muscat — 477,000

Pakistan
Karachi — 9,339,000
Lahore — 5,143,000
Faisalabad — 2,009,000
Islamabad — 529,000

Philippines
Manila — 9,933,000

Qatar
Doha — 264,000

Russia (Asian)
Novosibirsk — 1,400,000
Yekaterinburg — 1,314,000
Omsk — 1,177,000
Chelyabinsk — 1,111,000

Saudi Arabia
Riyadh — 2,776,000
Jeddah — 2,046,000

Singapore
Singapore — 4,131,000

Sri Lanka
Colombo — 642,000

Syria
Halab (Aleppo) — 1,813,000
Damascus — 1,394,000

Taiwan
Taipei — 2,720,000

Tajikistan
Dushanbe — 529,000

Thailand
Bangkok — 6,320,000

Turkey (Asian)
Ankara — 3,203,000
Izmir — 2,232,000

Turkmenistan
Ashgabat — 407,000

United Arab Emirates
Abu Dhabi — 904,000

Uzbekistan
Tashkent — 2,142,000

Vietnam
Ho Chi Minh City — 4,990,000
Hanoi — 2,464,000

Yemen
Sanaa — 927,000

International comparability of population data is limited by varying census methods. Where metropolitan population is unavailable, core city population is shown.

Gross Domestic Product is a measure of the total goods and services generated by a country. Generally, manufacturing, high-tech services, and specialized agricultural products add more value than raw materials and basic food stuffs. The high-tech and oil producing countries on the fringes of Asia are the exceptions in this generally poor continent.

Gross Domestic Product

GDP per capita

- Over $20,000
- $10,000 to $20,000
- $5,000 to $9,999
- $2,500 to $4,999
- Less than $2,500
- No data

Source: *World Factbook*, CIA, 2001

Electricity Use

Kuwait 14,377
United Arab Emirates 14,177
United States 12,407
Japan 7,470
Israel 5,372
China 851
India 442
Laos 31

KWh (kilowatt hours) per person per year

Source: *World Factbook*, CIA, 2001

Agriculture is the predominant land use in Asia, though only one-sixth of the land is arable. Wet grains, such as rice, are the principal crops of China and Southeast Asian countries. Dry grains, such as wheat, are grown in limited areas of Russia and China. A lack of modern farming methods, except in Japan, Russia, and Israel, has historically limited food production. However, production is increasing in some countries as governments supply the needed technology. The rugged land and climate in Northern, Central and Southwest Asia limits land use to nomadic herding. Here, animals supply food, shelter, clothing, and transportation.

Most Asian countries have an insignificant number of manufacturing jobs relative to other occupations. Japan, South Korea, Taiwan, China, and Singapore are exceptions.

Natural resources are Asia's most important export. The oil fields of Southwest Asia supply much of the World's energy needs. Southeast Asia supplies the World with its tin, and coal is plentiful in areas of Russia, China and India. The lack of processing facilities limits many Asian countries in the use of their resources.

Land Use and Resources

Predominant land use

- Commercial agriculture
- Nomadic herding
- Subsistence agriculture
- Primarily forestland
- Limited agricultural activity

Major resources

- Coal
- Natural gas
- Oil
- Forest products
- Au Gold
- Ag Silver
- Fe Iron ore
- U Uranium
- Al Bauxite
- Diamonds
- Other minerals
- Fishing
- Major manufacturing and trade centers

Asia has many climates. This can be expected on a landmass that covers an area from below the Equator to the Arctic Ocean and from the Mediterranean Sea to the Pacific Ocean. Weather conditions fluctuate from the sub-freezing temperatures and snow of the tundra climate in Northern Russia, through the more temperate humid continental climate, past the arid conditions of Southwest and Central Asia, and finally to the warm and wet zones of South and Southeast Asia.

See photographs taken in different kinds of climates on pages 24–25.

Verkhoyansk
Lowest recorded temperature, -90°F (-68°C), 1892

Tirat Tsvi
Highest recorded temperature,129°F (54°C)

Climate

Tropical wet	Humid subtropical
Tropical wet and dry	Humid continental
Arid	Subarctic
Semiarid	Tundra
Mediterranean	Highland

Annual Precipitation

Centimeters	Inches
Over 203	Over 80
152 to 203	60 to 80
102 to 152	40 to 60
51 to 102	20 to 40
25 to 51	10 to 20
Under 25	Under 10

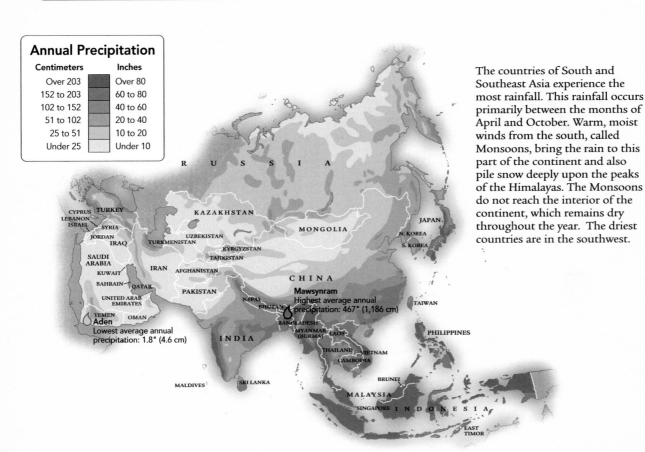

Mawsynram
Highest average annual precipitation: 467" (1,186 cm)

Aden
Lowest average annual precipitation: 1.8" (4.6 cm)

The countries of South and Southeast Asia experience the most rainfall. This rainfall occurs primarily between the months of April and October. Warm, moist winds from the south, called Monsoons, bring the rain to this part of the continent and also pile snow deeply upon the peaks of the Himalayas. The Monsoons do not reach the interior of the continent, which remains dry throughout the year. The driest countries are in the southwest.

Climate Graphs

ALMATY, Kazakhstan

BEIRUT, Lebanon

COLOMBO, Sri Lanka

DHAKA, Bangladesh

HONG KONG, China

JAKARTA, Indonesia

NEW DELHI, India

RIYADH, Saudi Arabia

TEHRAN, Iran

TIANJIN, China

TOKYO, Japan

YAKUTSK, Russia

Vegetation

- Unclassified highlands or ice cap
- Tundra and alpine tundra
- Coniferous forest
- Midlatitude deciduous forest
- Subtropical broadleaf evergreen forest
- Mixed forest
- Midlatitude scrub
- Midlatitude grassland
- Desert
- Tropical seasonal and scrub
- Tropical rain forest
- Tropical savanna

The continent's vegetation is as varied as its climate, ranging from the lush tropical vegetation of the South, Southeast, and East Asian countries to the sparse vegetation of Russia's vast arctic tundra.

See photographs of the different kinds of vegetation on pages 26–27.

Environmental Issues

- Current forest
- Cleared forest
- Area at highest risk of desertification
- Areas most affected by acid rain
- Poor air quality*

*Cities exceeding at least one of the World Health Organization's (WHO) annual mean guidelines for air quality

Sources: *Global Distribution of Original and Remaining Forests,* UNEP-WCMC, 2002
World Soil Resources Map Index, USDA/NRCS, 2002
World Development Indicators, World Bank, 1999

Asia's high population densities have led to a multitude of environmental problems, including pollution, deforestation, overfishing, and water shortages. With rapid population growth, pressures on land and water resources will only continue to increase. In western Asia, desertification and groundwater issues are the most pressing concerns. Most land in the region is either currently desert or is vulnerable to becoming desert in the future, and water is being withdrawn more quickly than it can be replaced.

Australia/Oceania

All islands east of 180° within the Republic of Kiribati observe the same date as the islands west of 180°, even though they are positioned on opposite sides of the International Date Line.

Maritime boundaries represented in the Pacific Ocean are not authoritative and are depicted merely to portray general zones of jurisdiction.

Facts

- Area: 3,300,000 square miles (8,547,000 square kilometers)
- Highest Point: Mt. Wilhelm, Papua New Guinea 15,400 ft. (4,694 m)
- Lowest Point: Lake Eyre, 52 ft. (16 m) below sea level
- Longest River: Murray-Darling, 2,510 mi. (4,039 km)
- Largest Lake: Lake Eyre, 3,500 sq. mi. (6,475 sq. km)
- Largest Country: Australia, 2,967,909 sq. mi. (7,686,850 sq. km)
- Largest City: Sydney, Australia, 3,997,000

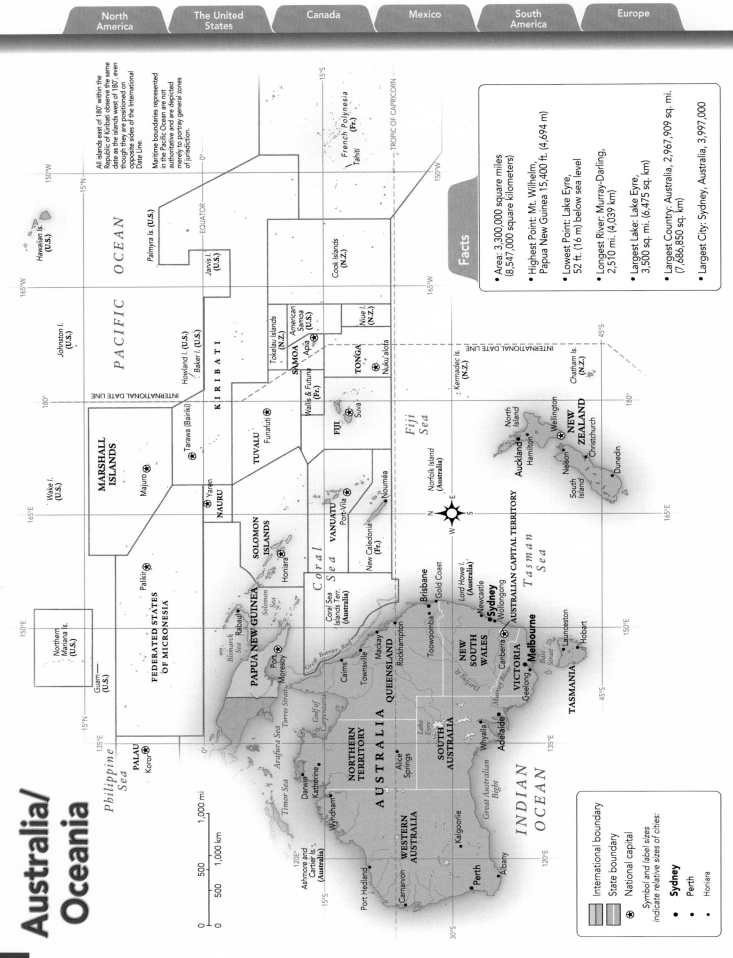

PACIFIC OCEAN

Hawaiian Is. (U.S.)

Palmyra Is. (U.S.)

Jarvis I. (U.S.)

Cook Islands (N.Z.)

French Polynesia Tahiti (Fr.)

TROPIC OF CAPRICORN

EQUATOR

Johnston I. (U.S.)

Howland I. (U.S.)
Baker I. (U.S.)

Wake I. (U.S.)

KIRIBATI

Tarawa (Bairiki)

INTERNATIONAL DATE LINE

Tokelau Islands (N.Z.)

American Samoa (U.S.)

SAMOA
Apia

Niue I. (N.Z.)

Wallis & Futuna (Fr.)

TONGA
Nuku'alofa

MARSHALL ISLANDS
Majuro

TUVALU
Funafuti

NAURU
Yaren

FIJI
Suva

Fiji Sea

Kermadec Is. (N.Z.)

INTERNATIONAL DATE LINE

Chatham Is. (N.Z.)

NEW ZEALAND
North Island
Wellington
Auckland
Hamilton
Nelson
Christchurch
South Island
Dunedin

Palikir

FEDERATED STATES OF MICRONESIA

SOLOMON ISLANDS
Honiara

VANUATU
Port-Vila

New Caledonia (Fr.)
Nouméa

Norfolk Island (Australia)

Tasman Sea

Northern Mariana Is. (U.S.)

Guam (U.S.)

PAPUA NEW GUINEA
Rabaul
Port Moresby

Bismarck Sea
Solomon Sea

Coral Sea

Coral Sea Islands Terr. (Australia)

Great Barrier Reef

Cairns
Townsville
Mackay
Rockhampton

Brisbane
Gold Coast

Lord Howe I. (Australia)

Newcastle
Sydney
Wollongong

AUSTRALIAN CAPITAL TERRITORY

PALAU
Koror

Philippine Sea

Torres Strait
Timor Sea
Arafura Sea

Gulf of Carpentaria

QUEENSLAND

Toowoomba

NEW SOUTH WALES

Canberra

VICTORIA
Melbourne
Geelong

Bass Strait

Launceston
Hobart

TASMANIA

Ashmore and Cartier Is. (Australia)

Darwin
Katherine
Wyndham

NORTHERN TERRITORY

AUSTRALIA

Alice Springs

Lake Eyre

SOUTH AUSTRALIA

Murray River
Darling R.

Whyalla
Adelaide

WESTERN AUSTRALIA

Port Hedland
Carnarvon

Kalgoorlie

Great Australian Bight

INDIAN OCEAN

Perth
Albany

Legend

- International boundary
- State boundary
- ⊛ National capital

Symbol and label sizes indicate relative sizes of cities:
- **Sydney**
- • Perth
- · Honiara

Scale: 0 — 500 — 1,000 mi
0 — 500 — 1,000 km

Elevation Profile

Major Metropolitan Areas

Australia
Sydney	3,997,000
Melbourne	3,367,000
Brisbane	1,628,000
Perth	1,340,000
Adelaide	1,073,000
Newcastle	471,000
Gold Coast (Southport)	397,000
Canberra	312,000

Fiji
Suva	167,000
Lautoka	29,000

Kiribati
Tarawa (Bairiki)	25,000

Marshall Islands
Majuro	18,000

Micronesia
Weno	15,000
Colonia	3,000

Nauru
Yaren	4,000

New Zealand
Auckland	1,075,000
Wellington	340,000
Christchurch	334,000

Palau
Koror	13,000

Papua New Guinea
Port Moresby	332,000
Lae	81,000
Madang	27,000
Wewak	23,000

Samoa
Apia	34,000

Solomon Islands
Honiara	61,000

Tonga
Nuku'alofa	30,000

Tuvalu
Funafuti	4,000

Vanuatu
Port-Vila	30,000

International comparability of population data is limited by varying census methods. Where metropolitan population is unavailable, core city population is shown.

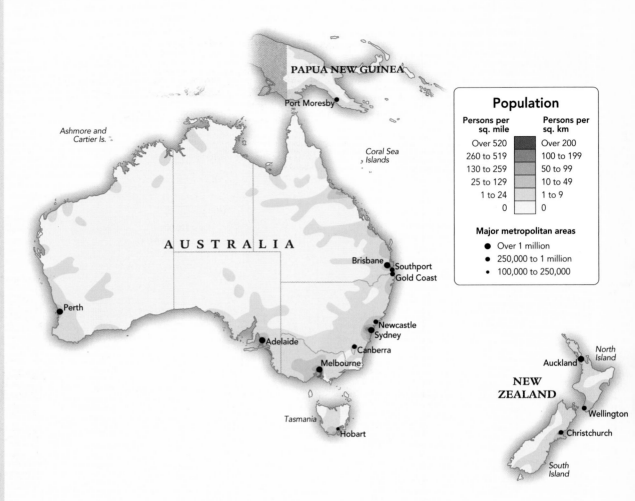

Population

Persons per sq. mile	Persons per sq. km
Over 520	Over 200
260 to 519	100 to 199
130 to 259	50 to 99
25 to 129	10 to 49
1 to 24	1 to 9
0	0

Major metropolitan areas
- Over 1 million
- 250,000 to 1 million
- 100,000 to 250,000

Estimated 2002 Population (in millions)
- Australia 20
- Papua New Guinea 5
- New Zealand 4
- All other countries 2

Source: U.S. Census Bureau

PAPUA NEW GUINEA

AUSTRALIA

Gross Domestic Product is a measure of the total goods and services generated by a country. Generally, manufacturing, high-tech services, and specialized agricultural products add more value than raw materials and basic food stuffs.

Australia derives its wealth and high standard of living from service industries and mineral extraction and processing. New Zealand's economy is oriented towards the export of animal products. Papua New Guinea's subsistence economy generates little excess wealth.

NEW ZEALAND

GDP of Island Nations

Fiji	Samoa
Kiribati	Solomon Islands
Marshall Islands	Tonga
Micronesia	Tuvalu
Nauru	Vanuatu
Palau	

Gross Domestic Product

GDP per capita

- Over $20,000
- $10,000 to $20,000
- $5,000 to $9,999
- $2,500 to a$4,999
- Less than $2,500
- No data

Source: *World Factbook*, CIA, 2001

Electricity Use

United States 12,407

Australia 9,211
New Zealand 9,134

Papua New Guinea 353

KWh (kilowatt hours) per person per year

Source: *World Factbook*, CIA, 2001

PAPUA NEW GUINEA

Ashmore and Cartier Is.

Coral Sea Islands

AUSTRALIA

Brisbane

Perth

Adelaide

Sydney

Melbourne

Tasmania

Land Use and Resources

Predominant land use

- Commercial agriculture
- Dairying
- Livestock ranching
- Primarily forestland
- Limited agricultural activity

Major resources

- Coal
- Natural gas
- Oil
- Forest products
- Au Gold
- Ag Silver
- Fe Iron ore
- U Uranium
- Al Bauxite
- Diamonds
- Other minerals
- Fishing
- ● Major manufacturing and trade centers

Auckland
North Island

South Island

NEW ZEALAND

...ustralia is rich in mineral ...esources. It ranks first in the min-...g of bauxite, diamonds, lead, and ...nc while being a leading producer ...f coal, gold, and iron ore. Its ura-...ium deposits are the largest in the ...orld, though largely undeveloped. ...odern methods of farming and ...rigation allow a very limited area ...f commercial agriculture to be ...ighly productive. Despite arid con-...tions, vast areas of the interior

support sheep and cattle grazing.

The New Zealand economy is built on livestock, raising more animals per person then any other country in the world. Meat and dairy products are important exports.

The economies of Papua New Guinea and the other island nations in the region rely primarily on subsistence agriculture and tourism.

Australia's climate is predominately warm and dry. The northern half of the country lies within the tropics and has very warm conditions year round. The southern half of the country lies below the tropics and experiences a warm summer and a cool winter.

New Zealand's climate is like that of the U.S. Pacific Northwest—mild and moist. Papua New Guinea and other island nations surrounding the equator have climates that are mainly very warm and moist year round.

See photographs taken in different kinds of climates on pages 24–25.

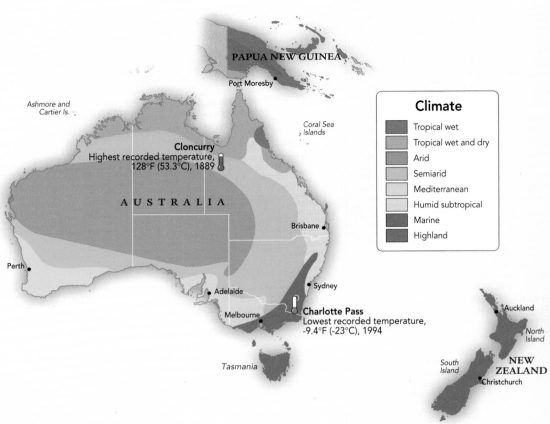

Climate
- Tropical wet
- Tropical wet and dry
- Arid
- Semiarid
- Mediterranean
- Humid subtropical
- Marine
- Highland

Cloncurry
Highest recorded temperature, 128°F (53.3°C), 1889

Charlotte Pass
Lowest recorded temperature, -9.4°F (-23°C), 1994

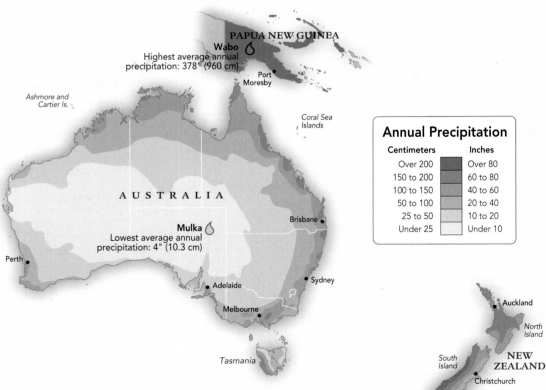

Annual Precipitation

Centimeters	Inches
Over 200	Over 80
150 to 200	60 to 80
100 to 150	40 to 60
50 to 100	20 to 40
25 to 50	10 to 20
Under 25	Under 10

Wabo
Highest average annual precipitation: 378" (960 cm)

Mulka
Lowest average annual precipitation: 4" (10.3 cm)

While Papua New Guinea and other island nations within the tropics receive plentiful and reliable rainfall, rain can be a problem in Australia—typically a case of feast or famine or bad timing. Westerly winds off of the Tasman Sea deposit precipitation on the mountain ranges of New Zealand, often in the form of snow that can be seen on some peaks year round.

Climate Graphs

Average daily temperature range (in °F)	Average monthly precipitation (in inches)
100° — High	20"
65° — Low	10"
32°	
0°	0"

BRISBANE, Australia

PERTH, Australia

AUCKLAND, New Zealand

PORT MORESBY, Papua New Guinea

ADELAIDE, Australia

MELBOURNE, Australia

SYDNEY, Australia

CHRISTCHURCH, New Zealand

Abundant Australian forestlands are limited to relatively narrow coastal regions where moisture, even if seasonal, is adequate. Most of the rest of the continent is covered by species of trees, bush, and grasses adapted to arid conditions. Eucalyptus are the most common trees in Australia.

Papua New Guinea has dense tropical rain forests, and New Zealand has mixed forests and grasslands arising from its temperate climate.

See photographs of different kinds of vegetation on pages 26–27.

Vegetation

- Subtropical broadleaf evergreen forest
- Mixed forest
- Midlatitude scrubland
- Midlatitude grassland
- Desert
- Tropical seasonal and scrub
- Tropical rain forest
- Tropical savanna

Environmental Issues

- Current forest
- Cleared forest
- Area at highest risk of desertification
- • Poor air quality*

*Cities exceeding at least one of the World Health Organization's (WHO) annual mean guidelines for air quality

Sources: *Global Distribution of Original and Remaining Forests*, UNEP-WCMC, 2002
World Soil Resources Map Index, USDA/NRCS, 2002
World Development Indicators, World Bank, 1999

Biodiversity loss (a decrease in the variety of life forms and ecosystems) is a leading environmental problem in both Australia and New Zealand. Over the past two hundred years, vast areas have been cleared for settlements and farmland. This land clearing, along with the introduction of non-native plant and animal species, has permanently altered the ecological balance. In New Zealand, it is estimated that eighty-five percent of the original lowland forests and wetlands have been lost due to human influences. Desertification, often brought on by overgrazing, is another serious environmental threat in many parts of Australia.

	Page	Latitude	Longitude
...nbia Mts., *mountains*	75	51°00'N	119°00'W
...bia Plat., *plateau*	54	45°00'N	118°00'W
...bus, GA	51	32°28'N	84°59'W
...bus, OH	51	39°58'N	83°00'W
...tán, *Mexico*	76	16°15'N	92°07'W
...odoro Rivadavia, *Argentina*	78	45°51'S	67°29'W
...orin, C., *cape*	97	8°00'N	78°00'E
...oros, *country*	90	12°00'S	43°00'E
...oros Is., *islands*	91	11°00'S	43°00'E
...kry, *Guinea*	90	9°31'N	13°42'W
...epción, *Chile*	78	36°48'S	73°02'W
...epción, *Paraguay*	78	23°23'S	57°25'W
...epción del Oro, *Mexico*	76	24°36'N	101°26'W
...eption, Pt., *cape*	54	34°00'N	120°00'W
...nos, *river*	77	29°00'N	105°00'W
...ord, NH	51	43°12'N	71°32'W
...o, *river*	91	2°00'N	22°00'E
...o Basin, *basin*	91	1°00'S	23°00'E
...nd, *river*	55	42°00'N	73°00'W
...ecticut, *state, U.S.*	51	42°00'N	73°00'W
...ance, L., *lake*	85	48°00'N	9°00'E
...anta, *Romania*	84	44°11'N	28°39'E
...ands, *dependency, N.Z.*	102	20°00'S	158°00'W
...Is., *islands*	103	20°00'S	158°00'W
...Mt., *peak*	103	44°00'S	170°00'E
...Str., *strait*	103	41°00'S	174°00'E
...hagen, *Denmark*	84	55°41'N	12°35'E
...pó, *Chile*	78	27°23'S	70°18'W
...Canyon, *canyon*	77	27°00'N	108°00'W
...Sea, *sea*	103	15°00'S	150°00'E
...Sea Islands Ter., *dependency, Austl.*	102	17°00'S	150°00'E
...ba, *Argentina*	78	31°23'S	64°11'W
...ba, *Spain*	84	37°53'N	4°47'W
...Ireland	84	51°54'N	8°28'W
...r Brook, *Canada*	74	48°57'N	57°57'W
...wall, *Canada*	74	45°02'N	74°45'W
...s Christi, TX	50	27°48'N	97°24'W
...entes, *Argentina*	78	27°30'S	58°49'W
...a, C., *cape*	77	20°00'N	106°00'W
...a, *island*	85	43°00'N	9°00'E
...ba, *Brazil*	78	19°01'S	57°38'W
...Rica, *country*	44	10°00'N	85°00'W
...d'Ivoire, *country*	90	5°00'N	5°00'W
...nel I., *island*	77	20°00'N	87°00'W
...rook, *Canada*	74	49°31'N	115°46'W
...., *lake*	75	57°00'N	108°00'W
...Sea of, *sea*	85	36°00'N	25°00'E
...a, *peninsula*	85	45°00'N	34°00'E
...a, *country*	84	45°00'N	15°00'E
...ro do Sul, *Brazil*	91	7°38'S	72°40'W
...o, *river*	91	15°00'S	22°00'W
...témoc, *Mexico*	76	28°25'N	106°51'W
...*country*	44	22°00'N	80°00'W
...ango, *river*	91	15°00'S	18°00'E
...ago, *Colombia*	78	7°53'N	72°29'W
...a, *Ecuador*	78	2°54'S	79°01'W
...avaca, *Mexico*	76	18°55'N	99°14'W
...á, *Brazil*	78	15°35'S	56°07'W
...án, *Mexico*	76	24°47'N	107°23'W
...ná, *Venezuela*	78	10°27'N	64°11'W
...er, *river*	55	37°00'N	88°00'W
...erland Pen., *peninsula*	75	66°00'N	65°00'W
...erland Plat., *plateau*	55	35°00'N	85°00'W
...erland Sound, *bay*	75	65°00'N	65°00'W
...ao, *island*	77	12°00'N	69°00'W
...oa, *Brazil*	78	25°27'S	49°16'W
...nelles, *strait*	85	13°32'S	71°56'W
...s, *islands*	85	37°00'N	25°00'E
...s, *country*	97	35°00'N	33°00'E
...., *island*	97	35°00'N	33°00'E
...Rep., *country*	84	49°00'N	15°00'E

	Page	Latitude	Longitude
...Senegal	90	14°42'N	17°27'W
...TX	50	32°47'N	96°48'W
...tia, *region*	91	21°00'S	19°00'E
...land, *region*	91	21°00'S	19°00'E
...cus, *Syria*	96	33°31'N	36°18'E
...ore, Cap, *cape*	91	12°00'S	48°00'E
...ng, *Vietnam*	96	16°03'N	108°12'E
...ie, *river*	85	49°00'N	10°00'E
...e Delta, *delta*	85	45°00'N	29°00'E
...Salaam, *Tanzania*	90	6°49'S	39°17'E
...g, *Australia*	102	12°25'S	130°53'E
...e-Kavir, *desert*	96	35°00'N	54°00'E
...vpils, *Latvia*	84	55°53'N	26°32'E
...ain, *Canada*	74	51°10'N	100°04'W
...., *Philippines*	96	7°04'N	125°36'E
...port, IA	51	41°31'N	90°35'W
...Sea, *sea*	15	65°00'S	95°00'E
...Str., *strait*	45	64°00'N	57°00'W
...k, *Canada*	74	64°04'N	139°24'W
...n Creek, *Canada*	74	56°00'N	120°15'W
...on, OH	51	39°46'N	84°12'W
...Sea, *depression*	97	31°00'N	35°00'E
...Val., *depression*	54	36°00'N	117°00'W
...cen, *Hungary*	84	47°32'N	21°37'E
...tur, IL	51	39°50'N	88°57'W
...Plat., *plateau*	97	23°00'N	79°00'E
...are, *river*	55	42°00'N	74°00'W
...are, *state, U.S.*	51	39°00'N	74°00'W
...are Bay, *bay*	55	39°00'N	75°00'W
...do, C., *cape*	55	41°00'N	70°00'W
...India	96	28°41'N	77°12'E
...as, *Mexico*	76	25°50'N	100°06'W
...., *Canada*	74	65°12'N	123°27'W
...cratic Rep. the Congo, *country*	90	1°00'S	21°00'E

	Page	Latitude	Longitude
Denakil, *region*	91	13°00'N	41°00'E
Denmark, *country*	84	56°00'N	10°00'E
Denmark Str., *strait*	45	65°00'N	31°00'W
Denver, CO	50	39°44'N	104°59'W
Dese, *Ethiopia*	90	11°10'N	39°37'E
Des Moines, IA	51	41°36'N	93°37'W
Des Moines, *river*	55	43°00'N	94°00'W
Desna, *river*	85	52°00'N	32°00'E
Detroit, MI	51	42°20'N	83°03'W
Devon I., *island*	75	76°00'N	85°00'W
Dhaka, *Bangladesh*	96	23°43'N	90°26'E
Diefenbaker, L., *lake*	75	50°00'N	107°00'W
Dijon, *France*	84	47°20'N	5°02'E
Dili, *East Timor*	96	8°35'S	125°36'E
Dinaric Alps, *mountains*	85	44°00'N	17°00'E
Dire Dawa, *Ethiopia*	90	9°36'N	41°52'E
Dirk Hartog I., *island*	103	26°00'S	113°00'E
Distrito Federal, *fed. dist., Mex.*	76	19°00'N	101°00'W
Djibouti, *country*	90	11°00'N	41°00'E
Djibouti, *Djibouti*	90	11°34'N	43°08'E
Dnieper, *river*	85	49°00'N	33°00'E
Dnieper Upland, *highlands*	85	49°00'N	32°00'E
Dniester, *river*	85	49°00'N	26°00'E
Dnipropetrovs'k, *Ukraine*	84	48°27'N	34°59'E
Dodoma, *Tanzania*	90	6°09'S	35°42'E
Doha, *Qatar*	96	25°15'N	51°26'E
Dominica, *country*	44	16°00'N	61°00'W
Dominican Rep., *country*	44	20°00'N	70°00'W
Don, *river*	85	48°00'N	40°00'E
Donets, *river*	85	49°00'N	38°00'E
Donets Basin, *basin*	85	48°00'N	38°00'E
Donets'k, *Ukraine*	84	48°01'N	37°48'E
Douala, *Cameroon*	90	4°03'N	9°43'E
Dourados, *Brazil*	78	22°14'S	54°48'W
Douro, *river*	85	43°00'N	7°00'W
Dover, DE	51	39°09'N	75°31'W
Dover, Str. of, *strait*	85	51°00'N	1°00'E
Drakensberg, *mountains*	91	30°00'S	30°00'E
Drake Passage, *strait*	14	60°00'S	70°00'W
Dresden, *Germany*	84	51°03'N	13°44'E
Dryden, *Canada*	74	49°47'N	92°49'W
Dubawnt, *river*	75	63°00'N	104°00'W
Dubawnt L., *lake*	75	63°00'N	100°00'W
Dublin, *Ireland*	84	53°21'N	6°16'W
Dubrovnik, *Croatia*	84	42°39'N	18°05'E
Duluth, MN	51	46°47'N	92°06'W
Dund-Us, *Mongolia*	96	47°59'N	91°39'E
Dunedin, *New Zealand*	102	45°52'S	170°30'E
Durango, *Mexico*	76	24°02'N	104°39'W
Durango, *state, Mex.*	76	24°00'N	104°00'W
Durban, *S. Africa*	90	29°50'S	31°01'E
Dushanbe, *Tajikistan*	96	38°34'N	68°48'E
Dzungarian Basin, *basin*	97	45°00'N	88°00'E

E

	Page	Latitude	Longitude
East China Sea, *sea*	97	29°00'N	124°00'E
Easter I., *dependency*	16	27°07'S	109°22'W
Easter I., *island*	14	27°07'S	109°22'W
Eastern Desert, *desert*	91	26°00'N	32°00'E
Eastern Ghats, *mountains*	97	15°00'N	82°00'E
East London, *S. Africa*	90	33°00'S	27°54'E
East Siberian Sea, *sea*	97	73°00'N	165°00'E
East Timor, *country*	96	9°00'S	125°00'E
Ebro, *river*	85	43°00'N	2°00'W
Ecuador, *country*	78	2°00'S	80°00'W
Edinburgh, *United Kingdom*	84	55°57'N	3°11'W
Edmonton, *Canada*	74	53°35'N	113°31'W
Edwards Plat., *plateau*	54	31°00'N	101°00'W
Egypt, *country*	90	26°00'N	29°00'E
Elba, *island*	85	43°00'N	10°00'E
Elbe, *river*	85	54°00'N	11°00'E
Elbert, Mt., *peak*	54	39°00'N	106°00'W
Elbrus, Mt., *peak*	85	43°00'N	42°00'E
Elburz Mts., *mountains*	97	36°00'N	53°00'E
Eldoret, *Kenya*	90	0°32'N	35°16'E
El Fashir, *Sudan*	90	13°38'N	25°21'E
El Khârga, *Egypt*	90	25°27'N	30°33'E
Ellesmere I., *island*	75	83°00'N	76°00'W
Elliot Lake, *Canada*	74	46°23'N	82°39'W
Ellsworth Land, *region*	15	76°00'S	90°00'W
Ellsworth Mts., *mountains*	15	80°00'S	85°00'W
El Obeid, *Sudan*	90	13°11'N	30°13'E
El Paso, TX	50	31°46'N	106°29'W
El Salvador, *country*	44	14°00'N	89°00'W
El Tigre, *Venezuela*	78	8°53'N	64°16'W
Emi Koussi, *peak*	91	19°00'N	21°00'E
Encarnación, *Paraguay*	78	27°20'S	55°52'W
Encounter Bay, *bay*	103	37°00'S	139°00'E
Enderby Land, *region*	15	70°00'S	40°00'E
England, *division, U.K.*	84	52°00'N	2°00'W
English Channel, *strait*	85	50°00'N	4°00'W
Ensenada, *Mexico*	76	31°52'N	116°37'W
Equatorial Guinea, *country*	90	2°00'N	11°00'E
Erg Chech, *desert*	91	24°00'N	3°00'W
Erie, PA	51	42°08'N	80°05'W
Erie, L., *lake*	45	43°00'N	83°00'W
Eritrea, *country*	90	18°00'N	38°00'E
Esfahan, *Iran*	96	32°39'N	51°39'E
Esmeraldas, *Ecuador*	78	0°57'N	79°40'W
Espírito Santo, *Brazil*	103	15°00'S	167°00'E
Esquel, *Argentina*	78	42°55'S	71°20'W
Essen, *Germany*	84	51°27'N	7°03'E
Estevan, *Canada*	74	49°08'N	103°00'W
Estonia, *country*	84	59°00'N	29°00'E
Ethiopia, *country*	90	8°00'N	40°00'E
Ethiopian Highlands, *plateau*	91	9°00'N	39°00'E
Etna, Mt., *peak*	85	38°00'N	15°00'E
Eugene, OR	50	44°03'N	123°05'W
Eugenia Pt., *cape*	77	28°00'N	115°00'W
Euphrates, *river*	97	33°00'N	42°00'E
Europe, *continent*	15	50°00'N	10°00'E
Evansville, IN	51	37°58'N	87°33'W
Everest, Mt., *peak*	97	27°59'N	86°56'E
Eyre, L., *lake*	103	29°00'S	137°00'E
Eyre Pen., *peninsula*	103	33°00'S	136°00'E

F

	Page	Latitude	Longitude
Fairbanks, AK	50	64°50'N	147°43'W
Faisalabad, *Pakistan*	96	31°24'N	73°04'E
Falcon Res., *lake*	77	27°00'N	99°00'W
Falkland Is., *dependency, U.K.*	78	52°00'S	59°00'W
Falkland Is., *islands*	79	52°00'S	59°00'W
Farewell, C., *cape*	45	60°00'N	44°00'W
Fargo, ND	50	46°53'N	96°47'W
Faro, *Canada*	74	62°16'N	133°24'W
Faroe Is., *dependency, Den.*	84	62°00'N	7°00'W
Faroe Is., *islands*	85	62°00'N	7°00'W
Faya-Largeau, *Chad*	90	17°56'N	19°07'E
Fear, C., *cape*	55	34°00'N	78°00'W
Federated States of Micronesia, *country*	102	6°00'N	150°00'E
Feira de Santana, *Brazil*	78	12°15'S	38°58'W
Fès, *Morocco*	90	34°04'N	4°58'W
Feuilles, R. aux, *river*	75	58°00'N	73°00'W
Fianarantsoa, *Madagascar*	90	21°27'S	47°04'E
Fiji, *country*	102	19°00'S	178°00'E
Fiji Sea, *sea*	103	27°00'S	177°00'E
Filchner Ice Shelf, *ice shelf*	15	80°00'S	40°00'W
Fimbul Ice Shelf, *ice shelf*	15	70°00'S	5°00'W
Finisterre, C., *cape*	85	43°00'N	9°00'W
Finland, *country*	84	66°00'N	26°00'E
Finland, G. of, *gulf*	85	60°00'N	26°00'E
Fitzroy, *river*	103	18°00'S	125°00'E
Flagstaff, AZ	50	35°12'N	111°39'W
Flattery, C., *cape*	54	48°00'N	125°00'W
Flinders, *river*	103	19°00'S	141°00'E
Flinders I., *island*	103	40°00'S	148°00'E
Flinders Ranges, *mountains*	103	32°00'S	139°00'E
Flin Flon, *Canada*	74	54°48'N	101°52'W
Flint, MI	51	43°01'N	83°41'W
Flint, *river*	55	31°00'N	84°00'W
Flint Hills, *hills*	55	38°00'N	97°00'W
Flint I., *island*	103	11°00'S	152°00'W
Florence, *Italy*	84	43°46'N	11°15'E
Florencia, *Colombia*	78	1°36'N	75°35'W
Floriano, *Brazil*	78	6°47'S	43°00'W
Florianópolis, *Brazil*	78	27°36'S	48°34'W
Florida, *state, U.S.*	51	29°00'N	82°00'W
Florida Keys, *islands*	55	25°00'N	82°00'W
Florida, Straits of, *strait*	45	24°00'N	82°00'W
Former Yugoslav Rep. of Macedonia, *country*	84	41°00'N	22°00'E
Fortaleza, *Brazil*	78	3°46'S	38°33'W
Fort Collins, CO	50	40°35'N	105°05'W
Fort Frances, *Canada*	74	48°38'N	93°23'W
Fort Lauderdale, FL	51	26°07'N	80°09'W
Fort McMurray, *Canada*	74	56°41'N	111°22'W
Fort McPherson, *Canada*	74	67°26'N	134°52'W
Fort Nelson, *Canada*	74	58°47'N	122°42'W
Fort Peck L., *lake*	54	48°00'N	107°00'W
Fort St. John, *Canada*	74	56°13'N	120°51'W
Fort Simpson, *Canada*	74	61°50'N	121°21'W
Fort Smith, AR	51	35°23'N	94°24'W
Fort Smith, *Canada*	74	60°00'N	111°57'W
Fort Worth, TX	50	32°44'N	97°19'W
Foxe Basin, *bay*	75	66°00'N	79°00'W
Foxe Pen., *peninsula*	75	65°00'N	78°00'W
France, *country*	84	47°00'N	2°00'E
Franceville, *Gabon*	90	1°39'S	13°34'E
Francistown, *Botswana*	90	21°12'S	27°32'E
Frankfort, KY	51	38°12'N	84°52'W
Frankfurt, *Germany*	84	50°07'N	8°41'E
Franz Josef Land, *islands*	97	81°00'N	55°00'E
Fraser, *river*	75	52°00'N	123°00'W
Fraser I., *island*	103	25°00'S	153°00'E
Fredericton, *Canada*	74	45°57'N	66°40'W
Freetown, *Sierra Leone*	90	8°27'N	13°13'W
French Guiana, *dependency, Fr.*	78	4°00'N	53°00'W
French Polynesia, *dependency, Fr.*	102	15°00'S	140°00'W
French Polynesia, *islands*	103	15°00'S	140°00'W
Fresnillo, *Mexico*	76	23°10'N	102°51'W
Fresno, CA	50	36°45'N	119°46'W
Fria, C., *cape*	91	18°00'S	12°00'E
Frisian Is., *islands*	85	54°00'N	6°00'E
Frobisher Bay, *bay*	75	64°00'N	66°00'W
Front Range, *mountains*	54	40°00'N	105°00'W
Fuerte, *river*	77	26°00'N	109°00'W
Fuji, Mt., *peak*	97	35°22'N	138°44'E
Funafuti, *Tuvalu*	102	8°37'S	179°07'E
Fundy, Bay of, *bay*	75	45°00'N	67°00'W
Fuzhou, *China*	96	26°04'N	119°18'E

G

	Page	Latitude	Longitude
Gabes, G. of, *gulf*	91	34°00'N	12°00'E
Gabon, *country*	90	0°00'	12°00'E
Gaborone, *Botswana*	90	24°38'S	25°55'E
Galápagos Is., *islands*	79	1°00'S	91°00'W
Galdhøpiggen, *peak*	85	62°00'N	8°00'E
Galveston Bay, *bay*	55	29°00'N	95°00'W
Gambia, *country*	90	12°00'N	18°00'W
Gander, *Canada*	74	48°57'N	54°36'W
Ganges, *river*	97	25°00'N	80°00'E
Gangetic Plain, *plain*	97	28°00'N	81°00'E
Gao, *Mali*	90	16°16'N	0°00'
Garonne, *river*	85	45°00'N	0°00'
Garoua, *Cameroon*	90	9°18'N	13°23'E
Garry L., *lake*	75	66°00'N	100°00'W
Gary, IN	51	41°36'N	87°21'W
Gaspé, *Canada*	74	48°50'N	64°30'W
Gaspé Pen., *peninsula*	75	49°00'N	65°00'W
Gdansk, *Poland*	84	54°22'N	18°38'E
Gedaref, *Sudan*	90	14°02'N	35°23'E
Geelong, *Australia*	102	38°11'S	144°23'E
Genesee, *river*	55	43°00'N	78°00'W
Geneva, *Switzerland*	84	46°12'N	6°09'E
Geneva, L., *lake*	85	46°00'N	7°00'E
Genoa, *Italy*	84	44°25'N	8°56'E
Geographe Bay, *bay*	103	33°00'S	115°00'E
George, *river*	75	57°00'N	77°00'W
Georgetown, *Guyana*	78	6°47'N	58°07'W
Georgia, *country*	84	43°00'N	43°00'E
Georgia, *state, U.S.*	51	33°00'N	83°00'W
Germany, *country*	84	52°00'N	11°00'E
Ghadamis, *Libya*	90	30°08'N	9°30'E
Ghana, *country*	90	9°00'N	2°00'W
Ghardaïa, *Algeria*	90	32°30'N	3°40'E
Gibraltar, *dependency, U.K.*	84	37°00'N	5°00'W
Gibraltar, Str. of, *strait*	85	36°00'N	6°00'W
Gibson Desert, *desert*	103	25°00'S	127°00'E
Gijón, *Spain*	84	43°32'N	5°41'W
Gila, *river*	54	33°00'N	112°00'W
Gilbert Is., *islands*	103	0°00'	173°00'E
Giza, *Egypt*	90	30°01'N	31°13'E
Glâma, *river*	85	60°00'N	11°00'E
Glasgow, *United Kingdom*	84	55°51'N	4°16'W
Gobi, *desert*	97	43°00'N	105°00'E
Godavari, *river*	97	19°00'N	78°00'E
Goiânia, *Brazil*	78	16°42'S	49°15'W
Gold Coast, *Australia*	102	27°57'S	153°23'E
Gold Coast, *region*	91	5°00'N	1°00'W
Gonder, *Ethiopia*	90	12°34'N	37°26'E
Good Hope, C. of, *cape*	91	35°00'S	18°00'E
Göteborg, *Sweden*	84	57°42'N	11°56'E
Gotland, *island*	85	57°00'N	18°00'E
Governador Valadares, *Brazil*	78	18°51'S	41°59'W
Grain Coast, *region*	91	6°00'N	10°00'W
Granada, *Spain*	84	37°11'N	3°36'W
Gran Chaco, *plain*	79	23°00'S	62°00'W
Grand, *river*	55	43°00'N	86°00'W
Grand Canyon, *canyon*	54	36°00'N	113°00'W
Grande, *river*	79	20°00'S	48°00'W
Grande Prairie, *Canada*	74	55°11'N	118°48'W
Grand Erg Occidental, *desert*	91	31°00'N	0°00'
Grand Erg Oriental, *desert*	91	31°00'N	8°00'E
Grand Falls-Windsor, *Canada*	74	49°00'N	55°35'W
Grand Forks, ND	50	47°55'N	97°02'W
Grand Rapids, MI	51	42°58'N	85°40'W
Granite Peak, *peak*	54	45°00'N	110°00'W
Graz, *Austria*	84	47°05'N	15°27'E
Great Artesian Basin, *basin*	103	22°00'S	141°00'E
Great Australian Bight, *bay*	103	34°00'S	130°00'E
Great Barrier I., *island*	103	36°00'S	175°00'E
Great Barrier Reef, *reef*	103	15°00'S	146°00'E
Great Basin, *basin*	54	40°00'N	117°00'W
Great Bear L., *lake*	75	65°00'N	120°00'W
Great Dividing Range, *mountains*	103	22°00'S	149°00'E
Greater Antilles, *islands*	45	18°00'N	75°00'W
Greater Khingan Range, *mountains*	97	45°00'N	118°00'E
Greater Sunda Is., *islands*	97	5°00'S	110°00'E
Great Falls, MT	50	47°30'N	111°18'W
Great Plains, *plain*	45	45°00'N	105°00'W
Great Salt L., *lake*	54	41°00'N	113°00'W
Great Salt Lake Desert, *desert*	54	41°00'N	114°00'W
Great Sandy Desert, *desert*	103	21°00'S	125°00'E
Great Slave L., *lake*	75	63°00'N	115°00'W
Great Victoria Desert, *desert*	103	28°00'S	128°00'E
Greece, *country*	84	39°00'N	22°00'E
Green, *river*	55	37°00'N	87°00'W
Green, *river*	54	42°00'N	110°00'W
Green Bay, WI	51	44°31'N	88°01'W
Greenland, *island*	45	75°00'N	40°00'W
Greenland (Kalaallit Nunaat), *dependency, Den.*	44	75°00'N	40°00'W
Greenland Sea, *sea*	15	80°00'N	10°00'W
Green Mts., *mountains*	55	44°00'N	73°00'W
Greensboro, NC	51	36°04'N	79°48'W
Grenada, *country*	44	12°00'N	62°00'W
Grijalva, *river*	77	17°00'N	93°00'W
Groote I., *island*	103	14°00'S	137°00'E
Groznyy, *Russia*	84	43°24'N	45°47'E
Guadalajara, *Mexico*	76	20°40'N	103°21'W
Guadalcanal I., *island*	103	10°00'S	160°00'E
Guadalupe I., *island*	77	29°00'N	118°00'W
Guadalupe Peak, *peak*	54	32°00'N	104°00'W
Guadeloupe, *dependency, Fr.*	44	18°00'N	62°00'W
Guadiana, *river*	85	39°00'N	8°00'W
Guajará-Mirim, *Brazil*	78	10°48'S	65°22'W
Guam, *dependency, U.S.*	102	13°00'N	145°00'E
Guam, *island*	103	13°00'N	145°00'E
Guanajuato, *Mexico*	76	21°00'N	101°17'W
Guanajuato, *state, Mex.*	76	22°00'N	101°00'W
Guangzhou, *China*	96	23°08'N	113°18'E
Guaporé, *river*	79	13°00'S	63°00'W
Guasave, *Mexico*	76	25°34'N	108°29'W
Guatemala, *country*	44	16°00'N	91°00'W
Guatemala City, *Guatemala*	44	14°37'N	90°31'W
Guayaquil, *Ecuador*	78	2°12'S	79°54'W
Guayaquil, G. of, *gulf*	79	3°00'S	80°00'W
Guaymas, *Mexico*	76	27°55'N	110°53'W
Guernsey, *island*	85	49°00'N	3°00'W
Guerrero, *state, Mex.*	76	17°00'N	101°00'W
Guerrero Negro, *Mexico*	76	27°58'N	114°03'W
Guiana Highlands, *plateau*	79	5°00'N	62°00'W
Guinea, *country*	90	11°00'N	12°00'W
Guinea, G. of, *gulf*	91	2°00'N	3°00'E
Guinea-Bissau, *country*	90	12°00'N	16°00'W
Guiyang, *China*	96	26°36'N	106°41'E
Gulf Coastal Plain, *plain*	55	30°00'N	93°00'W
Gurupi, *Brazil*	78	11°46'S	49°05'W
Guyana, *country*	78	7°00'N	59°00'W
Gwardafuy, C., *cape*	91	12°00'N	51°00'E
Gweru, *Zimbabwe*	90	19°28'S	29°49'E

H

	Page	Latitude	Longitude
Hainan, *island*	97	19°00'N	110°00'E
Haiti, *country*	44	19°00'N	73°00'W
Halifax, *Canada*	74	44°38'N	63°36'W
Halifax Bay, *bay*	103	19°00'S	147°00'E
Hall Pen., *peninsula*	75	65°00'N	66°00'W
Hamburg, *Germany*	84	53°33'N	10°01'E
Hamersley Range, *mountains*	103	23°00'S	118°00'E
Hamilton, *Canada*	74	43°16'N	79°51'W
Hamilton, *New Zealand*	102	37°47'S	175°18'E
Hammerfest, *Norway*	84	70°40'N	23°42'E
Hannover, *Germany*	84	52°22'N	9°45'E
Hanoi, *Vietnam*	96	21°02'N	105°49'E
Happy Valley-Goose Bay, *Canada*	74	53°00'N	60°23'W
Harare, *Zimbabwe*	90	17°49'S	31°03'E
Harbin, *China*	96	45°43'N	126°43'E
Hargeysa, *Somalia*	90	9°31'N	44°03'E
Harrisburg, PA	51	40°16'N	76°53'W
Hartford, CT	51	41°46'N	72°41'W
Hatteras, C., *cape*	55	35°00'N	75°00'W
Havana, *Cuba*	44	23°09'N	82°23'W
Havre-St-Pierre, *Canada*	74	50°15'N	63°36'W
Hawaii, *island*	50	21°00'N	158°00'W
Hawaii, *state, U.S.*	50	21°00'N	158°00'W
Hawaiian Is., *islands*	50	21°00'N	158°00'W
Hay, *river*	75	58°00'N	118°00'W
Hay River, *Canada*	74	60°49'N	115°46'W
Hearst, *Canada*	74	49°42'N	83°40'W
Hecate Str., *strait*	75	53°00'N	131°00'W
Helena, MT	50	46°36'N	112°02'W
Helsinki, *Finland*	84	60°11'N	24°56'E
Hermosillo, *Mexico*	76	29°04'N	110°55'W
Herrero, Pt., *cape*	77	19°00'N	87°00'W
Hidalgo, *state, Mex.*	76	21°00'N	99°00'W
Hidalgo del Parral, *Mexico*	76	26°56'N	105°41'W
Highlands, *mountains*	85	57°00'N	5°00'W
High Level, *Canada*	74	58°31'N	117°06'W
Hiiumaa I., *island*	85	59°00'N	22°00'E
Hilo, HI	50	19°44'N	155°05'W
Himalayas, *mountains*	97	29°00'N	86°00'E
Hindu Kush, *mountains*	97	35°00'N	71°00'E
Hispaniola, *island*	45	18°00'N	69°00'W
Hobart, *Australia*	102	42°48'S	147°18'E
Ho Chi Minh City, *Vietnam*	96	10°43'N	106°43'E
Hokkaido, *island*	97	44°00'N	143°00'E
Holman, *Canada*	74	70°43'N	117°41'W
Homel', *Belarus*	84	52°29'N	31°00'E
Honduras, *country*	44	17°00'N	85°00'W
Hong, *river*	97	23°00'N	104°00'E
Hong Kong, *China*	96	22°15'N	114°11'E
Honiara, *Solomon Islands*	102	9°19'S	159°44'E
Honolulu, HI	50	21°18'N	157°51'W
Honshu, *island*	97	37°00'N	140°00'E
Hood, Mt., *peak*	54	45°00'N	122°00'W
Hormuz, Str. of, *strait*	97	26°00'N	56°00'E
Horn, C., *cape*	79	56°00'S	68°00'W
Horn of Africa, *region*	91	9°00'N	47°00'E
Hotan, *China*	96	37°08'N	79°54'E
Houston, TX	51	29°46'N	95°22'W
Howland I., *dependency, U.S.*	102	1°00'N	177°00'W
Howland I., *island*	103	1°00'N	177°00'W
Hrodna, *Belarus*	84	53°41'N	23°51'E
Huajuapan de León, *Mexico*	76	17°48'N	97°47'W
Huambo, *Angola*	90	12°46'S	15°44'E
Huancayo, *Peru*	78	12°05'S	75°13'W
Huang (Yellow), *river*	97	36°00'N	111°00'E
Huánuco, *Peru*	78	9°54'S	76°16'W
Huascarán, Mt., *peak*	79	9°00'S	78°00'W
Hudson, *river*	55	42°00'N	74°00'W
Hudson Bay, *bay*	75	59°00'N	85°00'W
Hudson Str., *strait*	75	63°00'N	73°00'W
Hull, *Canada*	74	45°26'N	75°44'W
Humphreys Peak, *peak*	54	35°00'N	111°00'W
Hungary, *country*	84	47°00'N	19°00'E
Huntsville, AL	51	34°44'N	86°35'W
Huron, L., *lake*	45	45°00'N	82°00'W
Hyderabad, *India*	96	17°20'N	78°31'E

I

	Page	Latitude	Longitude
Iasi, *Romania*	84	47°10'N	27°36'E
Ibadan, *Nigeria*	90	7°24'N	3°53'E
Ibagué, *Colombia*	78	4°24'N	75°15'W
Iberian Pen., *peninsula*	85	41°00'N	4°00'W
Ibiza, *island*	85	39°00'N	1°00'E
Ica, *Peru*	78	14°03'S	75°45'W
Iceland, *country*	84	65°00'N	18°00'W
Iceland, *island*	85	65°00'N	18°00'W
Idaho, *state, U.S.*	50	44°00'N	114°00'W
Iguala, *Mexico*	76	18°21'N	99°32'W
Iguazú Falls, *falls*	79	26°00'S	55°00'W
Ilebo, *Dem. Rep. of Congo*	90	4°20'S	20°38'E
Ilhéus, *Brazil*	78	14°47'S	39°03'W
Illimani, Mt., *peak*	79	16°00'S	68°00'W
Illinois, *river*	55	41°00'N	90°00'W
Illinois, *state, U.S.*	51	41°00'N	89°00'W
Ilorin, *Nigeria*	90	8°29'N	4°33'E
Imperatriz, *Brazil*	78	5°32'S	47°29'W
I-n-Amenas, *Algeria*	90	28°03'N	9°34'E
India, *country*	96	23°00'N	79°00'E
Indiana, *state, U.S.*	51	40°00'N	86°00'W
Indianapolis, IN	51	39°46'N	86°09'W
Indian Ocean, *ocean*	15	10°00'S	80°00'E
Indochina Pen., *peninsula*	97	18°00'N	105°00'E
Indonesia, *country*	96	2°00'S	119°00'E
Indus, *river*	97	30°00'N	71°00'E
Infiernillo Res., *lake*	77	19°00'N	102°00'W
I-n-Salah, *Algeria*	90	27°12'N	2°31'E
Inuvik, *Canada*	74	68°22'N	133°42'W
Ionian Sea, *sea*	85	39°00'N	18°00'E
Iowa, *river*	55	43°00'N	93°00'W
Iowa, *state, U.S.*	51	42°00'N	93°00'W
Iqaluit, *Canada*	74	63°45'N	68°26'W
Iquique, *Chile*	78	20°13'S	70°10'W
Iquitos, *Peru*	78	3°45'S	73°11'W
Iraklio, *Greece*	84	35°20'N	25°08'E
Iran, *country*	96	31°00'N	57°00'E
Irapuato, *Mexico*	76	20°39'N	101°22'W
Iraq, *country*	96	32°00'N	41°00'E

Name	Page	Latitude	Longitude
Seward Pen., peninsula	54	65°00'N	165°00'W
Seychelles, country	90	9°00'S	52°00'E
Seychelles Is., islands	91	8°00'S	52°00'E
Sfax, Tunisia	90	34°47'N	10°46'E
Shackleton Ice Shelf, ice shelf	15	64°00'S	100°00'E
Shanghai, China	96	31°12'N	121°28'E
Shasta, Mt., peak	54	42°00'N	122°00'W
Shawinigan, Canada	74	46°33'N	72°45'W
Sheffield, United Kingdom	84	53°22'N	1°28'W
Shenyang, China	96	41°49'N	123°30'E
Sherbrooke, Canada	74	45°24'N	71°53'W
Shetland Is., islands	85	60°00'N	1°00'W
Shikoku, island	97	33°00'N	133°00'E
Shilka, river	97	52°00'N	105°00'E
Shiraz, Iran	96	29°37'N	52°32'E
Shreveport, LA	51	32°31'N	93°45'W
Siberia, region	97	64°00'N	98°00'E
Sicily, island	85	37°00'N	14°00'E
Sicily, Str. of, strait	85	37°00'N	12°00'E
Sidra, G. of, gulf	91	32°00'N	19°00'E
Sierra Azul, mountains	77	23°00'N	99°00'W
Sierra Leone, country	90	9°00'N	12°00'W
Sierra Madre de Chiapas, mountains	77	16°00'N	93°00'W
Sierra Madre del Sur, mountains	77	17°00'N	99°00'W
Sierra Madre Occidental, mountains	77	27°00'N	107°00'W
Sierra Madre Oriental, mountains	77	25°00'N	100°00'W
Sierra Morena, mountains	85	38°00'N	5°00'W
Sierra Nevada, mountains	54	38°00'N	120°00'W
Sierra San Pedro Mártir, mountains	77	32°00'N	116°00'W
Simferopol', Ukraine	84	44°58'N	34°06'E
Sinai Pen., peninsula	91	29°00'N	34°00'E
Sinaloa, state, Mex.	76	24°00'N	107°00'W
Sincelejo, Colombia	78	9°18'N	75°24'W
Singapore, country	96	1°00'N	104°00'E
Singapore, Singapore	96	1°18'N	103°51'E
Sioux City, IA.	51	42°30'N	96°24'W
Sioux Falls, SD	50	43°33'N	96°42'W
Siple I., island	15	74°00'S	135°00'W
Siwah, Egypt	90	29°11'N	25°31'E
Skagerrak, strait	85	58°00'N	9°00'E
Skeena, river	75	55°00'N	129°00'W
Skeleton Coast, region	91	22°00'S	12°00'E
Skopje, F.Y.R. Macedonia	84	42°00'N	21°25'E
Skovorodino, Russia	96	54°02'N	123°59'E
Slave, river	75	61°00'N	112°00'W
Slave Coast, region	91	6°00'N	2°00'E
Slovakia, country	84	48°00'N	19°00'E
Slovenia, country	84	47°00'N	15°00'E
Smallwood Res., lake	75	55°00'N	64°00'W
Smoky Hill, river	55	39°00'N	99°00'W
Smolensk, Russia	84	54°48'N	32°03'E
Snake, river	54	44°00'N	116°00'W
Snake River Plain, plain	54	43°00'N	115°00'W
Society Is., islands	103	18°00'S	152°00'W
Socotra, island	97	12°30'N	54°00'E
Sofia, Bulgaria	84	42°43'N	23°20'E
Sokoto, Nigeria	90	13°02'N	5°14'E
Solomon Islands, country	102	7°00'S	160°00'E
Solomon Islands, islands	103	9°00'S	165°00'E
Solomon Sea, sea	103	8°00'S	153°00'E
Somalia, country	90	4°00'N	45°00'E
Somali Pen., peninsula	91	10°00'N	49°00'E
Somerset I., island	75	74°00'N	95°00'W
Songea, Tanzania	90	10°41'S	35°39'E
Sonora, river	77	30°00'N	111°00'W
Sonora, state, Mex.	76	29°00'N	111°00'W
Sonoran Desert, desert	54	34°00'N	114°00'W
South Africa, country	90	30°00'S	21°00'E
South America, continent	14	10°00'S	50°00'W
Southampton I., island	75	65°00'N	85°00'W
South Australia, state, Austl.	102	32°00'S	135°00'E
South Bend, IN	51	41°41'N	86°15'W
South Carolina, state, U.S.	51	34°00'N	81°00'W
South China Sea, sea	97	14°00'N	115°00'E
South Dakota, state, U.S.	50	45°00'N	101°00'W
South East C., cape	103	44°00'S	147°00'E
Southern Alps, mountains	103	44°00'S	171°00'E
Southern Indian L., lake	75	57°00'N	98°00'W
South Georgia, island	79	54°00'S	37°00'W
South I., island	103	44°00'S	171°00'E
South Korea, country	96	35°00'N	128°00'E
South Orkney Is., islands	15	61°00'S	45°00'W
South Platte, river	54	40°00'N	104°00'W
South Pole, pole	15	90°00'S	0°00'
South Saskatchewan, river	75	51°00'N	110°00'W
South Shetland Is., islands	15	62°00'S	60°00'W
Spain, country	84	41°00'N	5°00'W
Spencer G., gulf	103	35°00'S	137°00'E
Split, Croatia	84	43°31'N	16°27'E
Spokane, WA	50	47°40'N	117°25'W
Springbok, S. Africa	90	29°40'S	17°54'E
Springfield, IL	51	39°48'N	89°39'W
Springfield, MO	51	37°13'N	93°18'W
Sri Lanka, country	96	7°00'N	81°00'E
Sri Lanka, island	97	7°00'N	81°00'E
Srinagar, India	96	34°11'N	74°48'E
Stanley, Falkland Is.	78	51°43'S	57°51'W
Stanovoy Range, mountains	97	56°00'N	130°00'E
Starbuck I., island	103	6°00'S	156°00'W
Stavanger, Norway	84	58°57'N	5°45'E
Steep Pt., cape	103	26°00'S	113°00'E
Stewart I., island	103	47°00'S	168°00'E
Stockholm, Sweden	84	59°20'N	18°02'E
Strasbourg, France	84	48°35'N	7°46'E
Stuttgart, Germany	84	48°48'N	9°11'E
Sucre, Bolivia	78	19°03'S	65°15'W
Sudan, country	90	11°00'N	29°00'E
Sudbury, Canada	74	46°29'N	81°00'W
Sudd, swamp	91	9°00'N	29°00'E
Sudeten Mts., mountains	85	51°00'N	16°00'E
Suez Canal, canal	91	31°00'N	34°00'E
Suez, G. of, gulf	91	28°00'N	34°00'E
Sukhona, river	85	60°00'N	42°00'E
Sulawesi (Celebes), island	97	2°00'S	121°00'E
Sumatra, island	97	0°00'	101°00'E
Sunda Str., strait	97	6°00'S	105°00'E
Sundsvall, Sweden	84	62°22'N	17°17'E
Superior, L., lake	45	47°00'N	86°00'W
Surabaya, Indonesia	96	7°13'S	112°44'E
Surgut, Russia	96	61°00'N	73°27'E
Suriname, country	78	4°00'N	57°00'W
Susquehanna, river	55	41°00'N	76°00'W

Name	Page	Latitude	Longitude
Sutlej, river	97	31°00'N	73°00'E
Suva, Fiji	102	17°48'S	178°32'E
Svalbard, islands	15	78°00'N	18°00'E
Swaziland, country	90	28°00'S	29°00'E
Sweden, country	84	61°00'N	15°00'E
Swift Current, Canada	74	50°17'N	107°47'W
Switzerland, country	84	46°00'N	8°00'E
Sydney, Australia	102	33°54'S	151°12'E
Sydney, Canada	74	46°09'N	60°12'W
Syktyvkar, Russia	84	61°47'N	51°02'E
Syracuse, NY.	51	43°03'N	76°09'W
Syr Darya, river	97	44°00'N	68°00'E
Syria, country	96	35°00'N	38°00'E
Syrian Desert, desert	97	32°00'N	40°00'E
Szczecin, Poland	84	53°26'N	14°33'E

T

Name	Page	Latitude	Longitude
Tabasco, state, Mex.	76	18°00'N	98°00'W
Tabora, Tanzania	90	5°01'S	32°49'E
Tabriz, Iran	96	38°05'N	46°15'E
Tacna, Peru	78	18°02'S	70°15'W
Tacoma, WA	50	47°15'N	122°27'W
Tademaït Plat., plateau	91	28°00'N	5°00'E
Tagus, river	85	40°00'N	8°00'E
Tahat, peak	91	24°00'N	5°00'E
Tahiti, island	103	18°00'S	149°00'W
Tahoe, L., lake	54	39°00'N	120°00'W
Taipei, Taiwan	96	25°04'N	121°33'E
Taiwan, country	96	24°00'N	121°00'E
Taiwan, island	97	24°00'N	121°00'E
Taiyuan, China	96	37°55'N	112°36'E
Tajikistan, country	96	39°00'N	71°00'E
Taklimakan Desert, desert	97	39°00'N	81°00'E
Talca, Chile	78	35°26'S	71°38'W
Tallahassee, FL	51	30°26'N	84°17'W
Tallinn, Estonia	84	59°24'N	24°44'E
Tamale, Ghana	90	9°24'N	0°50'W
Tamanrasset, Algeria	90	22°46'N	5°32'E
Tamaulipas, state, Mex.	76	24°00'N	99°00'W
Tamiahua Lagoon, bay	77	22°00'N	97°00'W
Tampa, FL	51	27°57'N	82°28'W
Tampa Bay, bay	55	28°00'N	83°00'W
Tampere, Finland	84	61°29'N	23°47'E
Tampico, Mexico	76	22°12'N	97°51'W
Tana, L., lake	91	12°00'N	38°00'E
Tanga, Tanzania	90	5°04'S	39°06'E
Tanganyika, L., lake	91	8°00'S	30°00'E
Tangier, Morocco	90	35°47'N	5°48'W
Tanzania, country	90	5°00'S	32°00'E
Tapachula, Mexico	76	14°54'N	92°15'W
Tapajós, river	79	5°00'S	57°00'W
Taranto, Italy	84	40°28'N	17°15'E
Taranto, G. of, gulf	85	39°00'N	19°00'E
Tarawa, island	103	1°00'N	173°00'E
Tarawa (Bairiki), Kiribati	102	1°19'N	172°58'E
Tarija, Bolivia	78	21°33'S	64°43'W
Tarim Basin, basin	97	40°00'N	83°00'E
Tartu, Estonia	84	58°22'N	26°42'E
Tashkent, Uzbekistan	96	41°14'N	69°16'E
Tasmania, island	103	42°00'S	147°00'E
Tasmania, state, Austl.	102	42°00'S	147°00'E
Tasman Sea, sea	103	38°00'S	159°00'E
Tatnam, C., cape	75	56°00'N	89°00'W
Taupo, L., lake	103	39°00'S	176°00'E
Taxco, Mexico	76	18°32'N	99°36'W
Taymyr Pen., peninsula	97	74°00'N	96°00'E
Tbilisi, Georgia	84	41°41'N	44°47'E
Tegucigalpa, Honduras	44	14°06'N	87°12'W
Tehran, Iran	96	35°41'N	51°26'E
Tehuacán, Mexico	76	18°28'N	97°24'W
Tehuantepec, G. of, gulf	77	15°00'N	95°00'W
Tehuantepec, Isth. of, isthmus	77	17°00'N	95°00'W
Tejupan, Pt., cape	77	18°00'N	104°00'W
Teles Pires, river	79	10°00'S	56°00'W
Temuco, Chile	78	38°44'S	72°36'W
Ténéré, region	91	19°00'N	12°00'E
Tennessee, river	55	35°00'N	86°00'W
Tennessee, state, U.S.	51	36°00'N	87°00'W
Tepic, Mexico	76	21°28'N	104°52'W
Teresina, Brazil	78	5°03'S	42°47'W
Términos Lagoon, bay	77	19°00'N	92°00'W
Tete, Mozambique	90	16°11'S	33°35'E
Texas, state, U.S.	50	31°00'N	99°00'W
Thabana Ntlenyana, peak	91	29°00'S	29°00'E
Thailand, country	96	16°00'N	102°00'E
Thailand, G. of, gulf	97	8°00'N	103°00'E
Thar Desert, desert	97	25°00'N	71°00'E
Thelon, river	75	64°00'N	104°00'W
The Pas, Canada	74	53°47'N	101°16'W
Thessaloníki, Greece	84	40°39'N	22°57'E
Thimphu, Bhutan	96	27°27'N	89°39'E
Thohoyandou, S. Africa	90	22°57'S	30°28'E
Thompson, Canada	74	55°44'N	97°51'W
Thunder Bay, Canada	74	48°26'N	89°14'W
Thurston I., island	15	72°00'S	100°00'W
Tianjin, China	96	39°07'N	117°10'E
Tian Shan, mountains	97	42°00'N	80°00'E
Tibesti Mts., mountains	91	21°00'N	19°00'E
Tibet, Plat. of, plateau	97	34°00'N	90°00'E
Tiburón I., island	77	29°00'N	113°00'W
Tierra del Fuego, island	79	54°00'S	68°00'W
Tigris, river	97	37°00'N	44°00'E
Tijuana, Mexico	76	32°31'N	117°03'W
Timan Ridge, highlands	85	66°00'N	50°00'E
Timisoara, Romania	84	45°46'N	21°14'E
Timmins, Canada	74	48°28'N	81°19'W
Timor, island	97	9°00'S	125°00'E
Timor Sea, sea	97	13°00'S	127°00'E
Tirana, Albania	84	41°20'N	19°49'E
Tisza, river	85	46°00'N	20°00'E
Titicaca, L., lake	79	16°00'S	69°00'W
Tizimin, Mexico	76	21°09'N	88°09'W
Tlaxcala, Mexico	76	19°19'N	98°14'W
Tlaxcala, state, Mex.	76	19°00'N	98°00'W
Toamasina, Madagascar	90	18°10'S	49°22'E
Tobruk, Libya	90	32°05'N	23°57'E
Tocantins, river	79	10°00'S	49°00'W
Togo, country	90	9°00'N	1°00'E
Tokelau Is., dependency, N.Z.	102	9°00'S	172°00'W
Tokelau Is., islands	103	9°00'S	172°00'W
Tokyo, Japan	96	35°40'N	139°45'E
Tolanaro, Madagascar	90	25°02'S	46°59'E
Toledo, OH	51	41°40'N	83°33'W
Toliara, Madagascar	90	23°21'S	43°39'E
Toluca, Mexico	76	19°18'N	99°39'W

Name	Page	Latitude	Longitude
Tombigbee, river	55	34°00'N	89°00'W
Tombouctou, Mali	90	16°45'N	3°02'W
Tomsk, Russia	96	56°28'N	84°59'E
Tonalá, Mexico	76	16°03'N	93°44'W
Tonga, country	102	20°00'S	175°00'W
Tonga, islands	103	20°00'S	175°00'W
Tongareva Is., islands	103	10°00'S	158°00'W
Toowoomba, Australia	102	27°34'S	151°59'E
Topeka, KS	51	39°03'N	95°41'W
Tornio, river	85	68°00'N	21°00'E
Toronto, Canada	74	43°39'N	79°23'W
Torreón, Mexico	76	25°32'N	103°27'W
Torres Str., strait	103	10°00'S	142°00'E
Tougouurt, Algeria	90	33°07'N	6°04'E
Toulon, France	84	43°08'N	5°57'E
Toulouse, France	84	43°38'N	1°28'E
Tours, France	84	47°24'N	0°41'E
Townsville, Australia	102	19°17'S	146°48'E
Trail, Canada	74	49°06'N	117°44'W
Transantarctic Mts., mountains	15	86°00'S	180°00'
Transcaucasia, region	85	42°00'N	45°00'E
Transylvanian Alps, mountains	85	46°00'N	23°00'E
Trenton, NJ	51	40°13'N	74°45'W
Trinidad, Bolivia	78	14°50'S	64°54'W
Trinidad, island	45	11°00'N	61°00'W
Trinidad and Tobago, country	44	11°00'N	61°00'W
Trinity, river	55	32°00'N	96°00'W
Tripoli, Libya	90	32°53'N	13°11'E
Tripolitania, region	91	30°00'N	13°00'E
Trois-Rivières, Canada	74	46°21'N	72°33'W
Tromsø, Norway	84	69°39'N	18°55'E
Trondheim, Norway	84	63°25'N	10°26'E
Trujillo, Peru	78	8°08'S	79°01'W
Truro, Canada	74	45°21'N	63°16'W
Tshikapa, Dem. Rep. of Congo	90	6°23'S	20°52'E
Tsimlyansk Res., lake	85	48°00'N	43°00'E
Tsumeb, Namibia	90	19°15'S	17°41'E
Tuamotu Arch., islands	103	17°00'S	141°00'W
Tucson, AZ	50	32°13'N	110°56'W
Tula, Russia	84	54°15'N	37°36'E
Tulsa, OK	51	36°09'N	96°00'W
Tumbes, Peru	78	3°35'S	80°26'W
Tunis, Tunisia	90	36°49'N	10°11'E
Tunisia, country	90	37°00'N	10°00'E
Turin, Italy	84	45°05'N	7°41'E
Turkana, L., lake	91	4°00'N	38°00'E
Turkey, country	84	38°00'N	36°00'E
Turkey, country	84	41°00'N	28°00'E
Turkmenistan, country	96	39°00'N	55°00'E
Turks and Caicos Is., dependency, (U.K.)	44	21°44'N	71°35'W
Turku, Finland	84	60°28'N	22°16'E
Tuvalu, country	102	8°00'S	178°00'E
Tuvalu, islands	103	8°00'S	178°00'E
Tuxpan, Mexico	76	20°57'N	97°26'W
Tuxtepec, Mexico	76	18°06'N	96°07'W
Tuxtla Gutiérrez, Mexico	76	16°45'N	93°05'W
Tver', Russia	84	56°54'N	35°53'E
Tyrrhenian Sea, sea	85	41°00'N	12°00'E

U

Name	Page	Latitude	Longitude
Ubangi, river	91	4°00'N	18°00'E
Uberlândia, Brazil	78	18°55'S	48°13'W
Ucayali, river	79	6°00'S	75°00'W
Uganda, country	90	2°00'N	33°00'E
Ukhta, Russia	84	63°36'N	53°51'E
Ukraine, country	84	49°00'N	29°00'E
Ulaanbaatar, Mongolia	96	47°56'N	106°53'E
Ulan-Ude, Russia	96	51°49'N	107°36'E
Ul'yanovsk, Russia	84	54°18'N	48°17'E
Umeå, Sweden	84	63°48'N	20°15'E
Umtata, S. Africa	90	31°33'S	28°42'E
Ungava Bay, bay	75	59°00'N	69°00'W
Ungava Pen., peninsula	75	61°00'N	74°00'W
United Arab Emirates, country	96	24°00'N	53°00'E
United Kingdom, country	84	54°00'N	0°00'
United States, country	44	39°00'N	98°00'W
Upper Pen., peninsula	55	46°00'N	87°00'W
Uppsala, Sweden	84	59°52'N	17°39'E
Ural, river	85	54°00'N	59°00'E
Ural Mts., mountains	85	57°00'N	59°00'E
Uruapan, Mexico	76	19°25'N	102°04'W
Uruguay, country	78	33°00'S	55°00'W
Uruguay, river	79	29°00'S	55°00'W
Ürümqi, China	96	43°47'N	87°37'E
Ushuaia, Argentina	78	54°47'S	68°15'W
Ustyurt Plat., plateau	97	43°00'N	55°00'E
Usumacinta, river	77	18°00'N	92°00'W
Utah, state, U.S.	50	39°00'N	112°00'W
Uzbekistan, country	96	42°00'N	69°00'E

V

Name	Page	Latitude	Longitude
Vaal, river	91	25°00'S	27°00'E
Vaasa, Finland	84	63°06'N	21°39'E
Valdai Hills, highlands	85	57°00'N	32°00'E
Valdés Pen., peninsula	79	43°00'S	64°00'W
Valdivia, Chile	78	39°47'S	73°13'W
Val-d'Or, Canada	74	48°07'N	77°47'W
Valencia, Spain	84	39°29'N	0°21'W

Name	Page	Latitude	Longitude
Valencia, Venezuela	78	10°11'N	67°58'W
Valera, Venezuela	78	9°19'N	70°38'W
Valladolid, Mexico	76	20°41'N	88°12'W
Valladolid, Spain	84	41°39'N	4°43'W
Valletta, Malta	84	35°54'N	14°31'E
Valparaíso, Chile	78	33°02'S	71°38'W
Vancouver, Canada	74	49°15'N	123°07'W
Vancouver I., island	75	49°00'N	127°00'W
Vänern, lake	85	59°00'N	13°00'E
Vanua Levu, island	103	16°00'S	179°00'E
Vanuatu, country	102	17°00'S	167°00'E
Varna, Bulgaria	84	43°12'N	27°55'E
Vatican City, country	84	42°00'N	12°00'E
Vatnajökull, glacier	85	64°00'N	16°00'W
Vättern, lake	85	58°00'N	14°00'E
Velikiy Novgorod, Russia	84	58°32'N	31°14'E
Venezuela, country	78	8°00'N	66°00'W
Venice, Italy	84	45°26'N	12°20'E
Veracruz, Mexico	76	19°00'N	96°08'W
Veracruz, state, Mex.	76	18°00'N	96°00'W
Verde, river	54	35°00'N	112°00'W
Verde, river	77	16°00'N	98°00'W
Verkhoyansk Range, mountains	97	65°00'N	130°00'E
Vermont, state, U.S.	51	44°00'N	73°00'W
Verona, Italy	84	45°26'N	11°00'E
Vert, Cap, cape	91	14°00'N	18°00'W
Vicebsk, Belarus	84	55°13'N	30°13'E
Victoria, Canada	74	48°26'N	123°22'W
Victoria, Seychelles	90	4°37'S	55°27'E
Victoria, state, Austl.	102	37°00'S	145°00'E
Victoria Falls, falls	91	19°00'S	26°00'E
Victoria I., island	75	72°00'N	109°00'W
Victoria, L., lake	91	1°00'S	33°00'E
Viedma, Argentina	78	40°51'S	62°59'W
Vienna, Austria	84	48°13'N	16°23'E
Vientiane, Laos	96	18°00'N	102°38'E
Vietnam, country	96	14°00'N	109°00'E
Vigo, Spain	84	42°13'N	8°44'W
Villa Ahumada, Mexico	76	30°37'N	106°30'W
Villahermosa, Mexico	76	17°59'N	92°55'W
Vilnius, Lithuania	84	54°41'N	25°16'E
Vinson Massif, mountains	15	78°00'S	88°00'W
Virginia, state, U.S.	51	38°00'N	79°00'W
Virginia Beach, VA.	51	36°51'N	75°59'W
Virgin Is., dependency, U.S./U.K.	44	18°00'N	65°00'W
Viscount Melville Sound, strait	75	75°00'N	108°00'W
Vistula, river	85	53°00'N	19°00'E
Viti Levu, island	103	18°00'S	178°00'E
Vladivostok, Russia	96	43°08'N	131°55'E
Volcán Misti, peak	79	16°00'S	72°00'W
Volga, river	85	57°00'N	35°00'E
Volga Delta, delta	85	46°00'N	48°00'E
Volga-Don Canal, canal	85	48°00'N	45°00'E
Volga Upland, highlands	85	52°00'N	45°00'E
Volgograd, Russia	84	48°45'N	44°30'E
Volgograd Res., lake	85	52°00'N	46°00'E
Volta, L., lake	91	8°00'N	0°00'
Volta Redonda, Brazil	78	22°28'S	44°04'W
Voronezh, Russia	84	51°36'N	39°24'E
Vychegda, river	85	62°00'N	47°00'E

W

Name	Page	Latitude	Longitude
Wabash, river	55	39°00'N	88°00'W
Waco, TX	50	31°33'N	97°09'W
Waddington, Mt., peak	75	52°00'N	126°00'W
Wake I., dependency, U.S.	102	19°00'N	167°00'E
Wake I., island	103	19°00'N	167°00'E
Wales, division, U.K.	84	52°00'N	5°00'W
Wallachia, region	85	45°00'N	24°00'E
Wallis and Futuna, dependency, Fr.	102	13°00'S	176°00'W
Wallis and Futuna, islands	103	13°00'S	176°00'W
Walvis Bay, Namibia	90	22°57'S	14°32'E
Warrego, river	103	27°00'S	145°00'E
Warsaw, Poland	84	52°15'N	20°59'E
Wasatch Range, mountains	54	40°00'N	111°00'W
Washington, DC	51	38°54'N	77°02'W
Washington, state, U.S.	50	46°00'N	121°00'W
Washington, Mt., peak	55	44°00'N	71°00'W
Watson Lake, Canada	74	60°09'N	128°46'W
Wau, Sudan	90	7°42'N	28°00'E
Wawa, Canada	74	47°59'N	84°45'W
Webi Jubba, river	91	5°00'N	42°00'E
Weddell Sea, sea	15	73°00'S	45°00'W
Wellesley Is., islands	103	16°00'S	140°00'E
Wellington, New Zealand	102	41°16'S	174°47'E
Weser, river	85	52°00'N	11°00'E
West Cape Howe, cape	103	35°00'S	118°00'E
West Dvina, river	85	57°00'N	25°00'E
Western Australia, state, Austl.	102	24°00'S	119°00'E
Western Ghats, mountains	97	13°00'N	75°00'E
Western Plat., plateau	103	25°00'S	125°00'E
Western Sahara, disputed territory, Mor.	90	25°00'N	15°00'W
West Ice Shelf, ice shelf	15	66°00'S	83°00'E
West Indies, islands	14	19°00'N	70°00'W
West Palm Beach, FL.	51	26°43'N	80°03'W
West Siberian Plain, plateau	97	61°00'N	79°00'E

Name	Page	Latitude	Longitude
West Virginia, state, U.S.	51	39°00'N	81°00'W
Wheeler Peak, peak	54	38°00'N	105°00'W
Wheeling, WV	51	40°04'N	80°43'W
White, river	55	35°00'N	91°00'W
White, river	55	39°00'N	87°00'W
White, river	44	44°00'N	101°00'W
Whitecourt, Canada	74	54°07'N	115°39'W
Whitehorse, Canada	74	60°44'N	135°04'W
White Mts., mountains	55	45°00'N	71°00'W
White Nile, river	91	12°00'N	32°00'E
White Sea, sea	85	66°00'N	36°00'E
Whitney, Mt., peak	54	37°00'N	119°00'W
Wholdaia L., lake	75	60°00'N	105°00'W
Whyalla, Australia	102	33°01'S	137°34'E
Wichita, KS	50	37°42'N	97°20'W
Wilhelm, Mt., peak	103	6°00'S	145°00'E
Wilkes Land, region	15	70°00'S	120°00'E
Williams Lake, Canada	74	52°09'N	122°09'W
Williston L., lake	75	56°00'N	135°00'W
Wilmington, DE.	51	39°45'N	75°33'W
Windhoek, Namibia	90	22°33'S	17°04'E
Windsor, Canada	74	42°18'N	83°02'W
Windward Is., islands	45	14°00'N	61°00'W
Winisk, river	75	55°00'N	88°00'W
Winnipeg, Canada	74	49°54'N	97°09'W
Winnipeg, L., lake	75	53°00'N	98°00'W
Winnipegosis, L., lake	75	53°00'N	100°00'W
Winston-Salem, NC.	51	36°06'N	80°15'W
Wisconsin, river	55	45°00'N	90°00'W
Wisconsin, state, U.S.	51	44°00'N	89°00'W
Wollaston L., lake	75	58°00'N	104°00'W
Wollongong, Australia	102	34°24'S	150°50'E
Woods, L. of the, lake	55	49°00'N	95°00'W
Worcester, MA	51	42°16'N	71°48'W
Wrangel I., island	97	71°00'N	180°00'
Wrath, C., cape	85	58°00'N	5°00'W
Wroclaw, Poland	84	51°06'N	17°02'E
Wuhan, China	96	30°32'N	114°18'E
Wyndham, Australia	102	15°29'S	128°08'E
Wyoming, state, U.S.	50	43°00'N	107°00'W

X

Name	Page	Latitude	Longitude
Xai-Xai, Mozambique	90	25°03'S	33°39'E
Xalapa, Mexico	76	19°32'N	96°54'W
Xi, river	97	24°00'N	110°00'E
Xi'an, China	96	34°17'N	108°55'E
Xingu, river	79	7°00'S	52°04'W

Y

Name	Page	Latitude	Longitude
Yablonovyy Range, mountains	97	53°00'N	115°00'E
Yakutsk, Russia	96	62°04'N	129°43'E
Yamoussoukro, Côte d'Ivoire	90	6°45'N	5°17'W
Yangon (Rangoon), Myanmar	96	16°49'N	96°10'E
Yaoundé, Cameroon	90	3°52'N	11°31'E
Yaqui, river	77	28°00'N	110°00'W
Yaren, Nauru	102	0°31'S	166°55'E
Yarmouth, Canada	74	43°48'N	66°07'W
Yaroslavl', Russia	84	57°36'N	39°51'E
Yazoo, river	55	33°00'N	90°00'W
Yekaterinburg, Russia	96	56°51'N	60°36'E
Yellowknife, Canada	74	62°29'N	114°22'W
Yellow Sea, sea	97	34°00'N	123°00'E
Yellowstone, river	54	46°00'N	108°00'W
Yellowstone L., lake	54	44°00'N	110°00'W
Yemen, country	96	15°00'N	47°00'E
Yenisey, river	97	67°00'N	84°00'E
Yerevan, Armenia	84	40°04'N	44°29'E
Yokohama, Japan	96	35°27'N	139°39'E
York, C., cape	103	11°51'S	142°00'E
Yorkton, Canada	74	51°12'N	102°26'W
Yucatán, state, Mex.	76	21°00'N	89°00'W
Yucatán Channel, strait	77	22°00'N	86°00'W
Yucatán Pen., peninsula	77	20°00'N	89°00'W
Yukon, river	45	65°00'N	150°00'W
Yukon Terr., territory, Can.	74	65°00'N	138°00'W
Yuma, AZ	50	32°44'N	114°37'W
Yumen, China	96	39°52'N	97°37'E

Z

Name	Page	Latitude	Longitude
Zacatecas, Mexico	76	22°46'N	102°33'W
Zacatecas, state, Mex.	76	24°00'N	103°00'W
Zagreb, Croatia	84	45°49'N	16°00'E
Zagros Mts., mountains	97	30°00'N	50°00'E
Zambezi, river	91	15°00'S	35°00'E
Zambia, country	90	15°00'S	26°00'E
Zanzibar, Tanzania	90	6°10'S	39°11'E
Zanzibar I., island	91	6°00'S	39°00'E
Zaporizhzhia, Ukraine	84	47°44'N	35°13'E
Zapotlán, Pt., cape	77	19°00'N	95°00'W
Zaragoza, Spain	84	41°39'N	0°53'W
Zaria, Nigeria	90	11°06'N	7°42'E
Zeil, Mt., peak	103	23°00'S	133°00'E
Zhengzhou, China	96	34°47'N	113°42'E
Zimbabwe, country	90	19°00'S	29°00'E
Zinder, Niger	90	13°48'N	8°59'E
Zürich, Switzerland	84	47°23'N	8°33'E

Abbreviations

Arch.	Archipelago
Austl.	Australia
Bos. & Her.	Bosnia & Herzegovina
C.	Cape
Can.	Canada
Cen. African Rep.	Central African Republic
Czech Rep.	Czech Republic
Dem. Rep. of Congo	Democratic Republic of Congo
Den.	Denmark
Dominican Rep.	Dominican Republic
fed. dist.	Federal District
Fed. States of Micronesia	Federated States of Micronesia
Fr.	France
Ft.	Fort
F.Y.R. Macedonia	Former Yugoslav Republic of Macedonia
G.	Gulf
Gr.	Greece
I.	Island
Is.	Islands
Isth.	Isthmus
It.	Italy
L.	Lake
Liecht.	Liechtenstein
Mex.	Mexico
Mor.	Morocco
Mt.	Mount
Mtn.	Mountain
Mts.	Mountains
N. Korea	North Korea
N.Z.	New Zealand
Pen.	Peninsula
Plat.	Plateau
Pt.	Point
R.	River
Rep.	Republic
Rep. of the Congo	Republic of the Congo
Res.	Reservoir
Russ.	Russia
Serb. & Mont.	Serbia and Montenegro
S. Africa	South Africa
S. Korea	South Korea
Sp.	Spain
St., St-	Saint
Ste., Ste-	Sainte
Str.	Strait
Terr.	Territory
U.K.	United Kingdom
U.S.	United States
Val.	Valley

For U.S. two-letter state abbreviations, see pages 52–53.